Gregory David Robert

The Mountain Shadow

album *Love&Faith*.

C000213435

—

THE
SPIRITUAL
PATH

GREGORY DAVID
ROBERTS

ABACUS

First published in Switzerland in 2021 by Empathy Arts SA
First published in Great Britain in 2021 by Little, Brown

1 3 5 7 9 10 8 6 4 2

A CIP catalogue record for this book
is available from the British Library.

ISBN 978-0-349-14467-2

Printed and bound in Great Britain by Clays Ltd, Elcograf S.p.A

Papers used by Abacus are from well-managed forests
and other responsible sources.

Abacus
An imprint of
Little, Brown Book Group
Carmelite House
50 Victoria Embankment
London EC4Y 0DZ

An Hachette UK Company
www.hachette.co.uk

www.littlebrown.co.uk

Contents

Introduction

When I started to write this, I realized that in part I was writing it to my younger Self – that always-searching but often selfish, frustrated, angered or even harmful Self. If my younger Self had read this book or one like it, it might've helped to spare some of my harm and negativity from the worlds and people I knew, and from my Self. And it might've helped me to set the compass to my own true North, just as walking the spiritual Path saved my much older Self from the downward spiral of grief, guilt and depression. So, this is for all the searching Selves we are, or were, or will become.

Everyone is spiritual. Everyone is on the spiritual Path.

Whether we know it or not we're all on the Path, we all find our ways to spiritual connection naturally, and many of us connect without ever striving for it.

But it's also possible to walk the Path consciously, with awareness and active commitment.

Six years ago, I had the motive, the means and the opportunity to walk consciously on the spiritual Path.

The *motive* was that I wanted to know – after decades of research into theology, mystical traditions and the spiritual, I wanted to know: is there something there? Is there some kind of Spiritual Reality, or not?

The *means* was a conch shell – my spiritual teacher had assured me that blowing the conch shell with utmost Innocence and sincerity in active, physical Devotion could, and would, connect me with the spiritual.

The *opportunity* came at a time in my life when I could go off the grid and focus a great part of my attention and energy to the attempt at active connection.

So, I did.

I took the steps that personal studies and my spiritual teacher had informed me were necessary in the sincere, authentic journey on the spiritual Path: Acknowledgment, Surrender and Devotion. I went off the grid and stopped going to lunches, dinners, parties, events, festivals, concerts, cinemas, theatres and just about everywhere else. I renounced many of my favorite things and focused on trying to be worthy of walking the Path. And then I blew the conch shell with my utmost sincerity twice a day, every day, in active and strenuous Devotion, for six years.

This is what happened.

GDR
March 23rd 2020
Oracabessa, Jamaica

The logic that I needed at the beginning, and that I followed into active Devotion, went like this:

First, I took it as accepted that the atheist position didn't make any sense: if there's even one thing in this universe that has metaphysical, or beyond-physical, characteristics, it makes no sense to deny the metaphysical altogether.

As it happens, there actually *is* something in our Universe that has both physical properties *and* metaphysical properties, and that is a photon of light.

Every scientist agrees that a photon of light has no mass, meaning that it doesn't weigh anything, and that it has no volume, meaning that it doesn't take up any physical space. A photon of light also has a unique relationship to time. So, a photon is there, but it's not there – not in the way that everything else with mass and volume are there. These are metaphysical characteristics.

Of course, the photon of light is really there, and we can bounce photons of light off mirrors and feel the energy effects when we concentrate them, but when it comes to describing what a photon of light *is*, the language of the metaphysical is the only one that applies: it's really there, yes, but, er, it doesn't weigh anything and it doesn't take up any space. It's also travelling at the speed of light, which nothing else can do. And, oh yeah, any two of those photons can react to one another simultaneously even when separated by the entire width of the observable Universe.

We can list those characteristics, and make calculations and theories based on them, but explaining how something is there but not there, travelling at impossible speed and changing in tandem across cosmic distances, requires an understanding that is beyond-the-physical, or metaphysical.

And even if just one thing in our Universe has metaphysical properties, such as a photon of light, it doesn't make sense to deny the metaphysical altogether. We just have to do a better job of defining it.

So, I recognized that the metaphysical is real, at least when it comes to photons of light, and began with an open mind.

Secondly, I wasn't thinking in terms of religion, but in terms of the spiritual.

I've prayed with believers in synagogues, mosques, temples, churches, gurdwaras, stupas, fire temples, caves and stone circles. I learned religious prayers in three languages and had the innocent joy of reciting them with friends when they invited me. I was an altar boy serving in the Catholic mass, my spiritual teacher is a Brahmin tantric Hindu, and I've studied at the feet of other religious teachers, but I'm not religious and I don't belong to any religion.

For my purpose, religion is what we *believe and accept* to be true, and the spiritual is *what we experience as true*.

Similarly, I didn't set out to investigate or study God. I don't know anything about God, and I'm always cautious whenever I hear someone say: "God wants you to do this ..." or "God says this or that ..."

God is by definition so huge, so immense beyond imagination, that I don't think anyone can know anything about God *directly*. It would be like matter and antimatter colliding, so to speak, leading to our annihilation.

How can we hope to see or directly experience the Divine source of all the Suns in all the Universes, when we can't stare at our own Sun for five minutes without destroying our vision?

So, if it's accepted for argument that such a Divine Perfection exists, I didn't think it would be logically possible to know that perfection, God, *directly*, but I reasoned that it might be possible to know such a Divine Perfection tangentially, *indirectly*.

For my purpose, the spiritual is not God.

The spiritual is the *spirit* of God in this worldly, material Universe.

Although God, if existing at all, is far beyond our limited human capacity to comprehend and know directly, there are some things that we can legitimately conjecture about our humble, human *concept* of such a Divine entity.

If we are to accept for the sake of argument that God exists, then that Divine entity would by definition be perfect, and *would do everything perfectly*. In fact, it would be logically inconsistent for God, or the concept of God, to be imperfect in any way, or to do anything imperfectly. All the major religions agree on this point, though they may differ on many others.

For this reason, in the logic system I developed for my Self to make the leap of Faith, I used the term *the Divine Perfection* instead of the term God: to keep the focus on the *perfect* nature of the Divine, and to avoid the many specific religious interpretations of what the word "God" means.

In the Material Reality that we know in everyday life, Perfection is an idea, a concept, and there is no such thing as Perfection: everything is imperfect in some way, and sometimes the appeal or poignancy of a thing is found in that sublime imperfection.

We use the word *perfect* imprecisely to say that something is complete, and without defect of any kind. But we also know that *nothing* is *absolutely* without imperfection: we use the word as an approximation.

In the spiritual language, however, Perfection is an absolute: it is absolutely Immaculate and absolutely without blemish, defect, exception, comparison or duplicate. Perfection is a singularity: all things, except for it, are imperfect in some way, and there can only be one.

To make this point in a different way, if we establish that someone is the tallest person in a room full of people, by definition every other person in the room is not the tallest.

When we establish a conceptual absolute, like Perfection, it means that by definition everything else *isn't* Perfection. The singular nature of Perfection is baked into the concept: there can be only one Perfection, otherwise the concept doesn't make sense.

Like the concept of Infinity, this is something that can only be accepted spiritually or philosophically, because such Perfection is unattainable in the Material Reality that we know as daily life: it doesn't exist, except in our minds as a concept, or as something we attribute to the inner essence of the Divine Perfection.

So, my logic ran, if there is a Divine Perfection, and if the Divine Perfection does everything *perfectly*, it follows that it is not within *the logic of that Perfection* for the Divine Perfection to destroy.

If the Divine Perfection could logically destroy, the Divine Perfection would destroy *perfectly*, and there would be nothing but the Divine Perfection.

But there is a lot of stuff, perhaps even a Multiverse of Universes of stuff, so therefore the Divine Perfection must be creative, not destructive. And all that we see around us in the perceivable Universe is an expression of the Divine Perfection's perfect Creativity.

Similarly, it can't be within the logic system of Perfection for the Divine Perfection to be a "taker."

If the Divine Perfection could logically take, the Divine Perfection would take perfectly, and there would be nothing but the Divine Perfection.

But there is a lot of stuff, so therefore the Divine Perfection must be a Giver, and all that we see in the perceivable Universe is an expression of the Divine Perfection's perfect Giving.

There's an emotional response in us that asks how we can accept the concept of such Divine Giving, when the world seems to have so much suffering and hardship everywhere? How can all this pain, hardship and misery be an expression of Divine Giving?

First, pain is the price of life, and speaking as someone who has known a lot of pain, I think that's a fair bargain for all the other amazing good that existence brings.

Second, it seems that when the Divine Perfection creates a Multiverse of matter, space and energy from nothing but God-stuff, so to speak, the movement from the perfect Divine nature to imperfect Nature requires many violent processes within the stars and planets and within the bodies of living things that emerge from the creation process. So, this is just how it is: the journey from the mind of God, so to speak, to the Material, Quantum and Spiritual Realities releases energies, forces and matter in this way.

Existence, for us, means the possibility of earth-quakes, volcanoes, hurricanes, cyclones, tornadoes, tsunamis and lots of other scary things. This is the way it must be, when the Divine Perfection creates imperfection, and once again, it seems to me a fair bargain.

And third, speaking from personal experience, I think that most of our human suffering is a beast of our own creation. Those were my sins, not God's. The unfairness and iniquity in the world are on us, not the Divine Perfection, and within our means to change.

My logic ran that as material beings in the Mate-rial Reality, it isn't logically possible for us to "know" the Divine Perfection in the same way that we would know any material thing.

However, I reasoned that it is logically permis-sible that the Divine Perfection, having imbued this

Universe with a Quantum Reality and a Material Reality, might also have imbued this Universe (or Multiverse) with a third reality of a spiritual nature, a Divine tendency field, with which we might connect: a Spiritual Reality.

It seemed to me reasonable that a Divine Perfection, creating everything from a perfect, Giving Creativity, would imbue the Universe with a spiritual component that, although not the Divine Perfection Itself, may provide a conduit or wavelength for indirect connection to The Source.

I wonder, now, that I went to so much trouble to create an intellectual or logical scaffold to climb on for the leap of Faith, when the leap itself took care of everything. I was applying the kind of thinking that studies the motorcycle manual thoroughly, and then takes on the repair or replacement of a component. But as I discovered, the encounter with the spiritual *writes its own manual* as we walk on the Path, and all the logical preparation becomes just so many blurred reflections in a smoky mirror.

Nevertheless, I needed something to hold on to before the leap: a framework of thought that could allow me to say *Hello* to the Divine Perfection authentically and sincerely, without feeling like a fool or a fraud.

So, the logic pathway wound on.

My studies had shown that many traditions and texts allude to the existence of this different Spiritual Reality, running parallel with or interwoven with the Material Reality of billiard balls, people and planets, and with the Quantum Reality of probability states, Schrödinger's Feline and quantum entanglement.

My logic ran that if such a thing as the Spiritual Reality were to exist, one way to connect with it might be through Giving, because the entire Multiverse of Universes is an expression of the Divine Perfection's perfect Giving.

Love is Selfless Giving.
Devotion is Selfless spiritual Giving.

Thus, by Giving spiritually in sincere Devotion, I reasoned that it might be possible to tune into the *wavelength or frequency of connection*, so to speak, with the Spiritual Reality.

This, then, was the logic key that I needed: to focus my Devotion on Giving, and not asking for anything, in a sincere attempt to establish a connection with the Spiritual Reality, should such a thing exist.

But before I could blow the conch shell for the first time and try to connect, the many texts and teachers I'd consulted over the decades had assured me that I had to follow three important and necessary steps on the Path – Acknowledgement, Surrender and Devotion – to do my utmost to be worthy of the connection, and I had to adjust my thinking to reflect the new and very different logic of the Spiritual Reality.

THE SPIRITUAL REALITY

My starting point was that if there is a Divine Perfection, and if that Divine Perfection's perfect Creativity created a Multiverse capable of evolving sentient beings, who are themselves capable of Acknowledgement, Surrender and Devotion, then that Divine Perfection might imbue that Universe with a Spiritual Reality, providing the capacity for spiritual connection within this Material Reality: within the lives we live in the everyday world we know.

I don't want to convince anyone of this, or of anything else. I'm simply describing the logic path that allowed me to 'leap' into the unknowable and commit my Self. It was the only thing that made sense to me.

In these pages I make statements about spiritual matters from time to time as if they're facts, but it's just my way of expressing myself. It's all opinion, and I don't ask or expect anyone to agree.

It seemed to me that if there is a non-material Spiritual Reality, it follows that the rules of logic would be unique, just as they are unique for the Quantum and Material Realities.

For example, in the Material Reality, things are either particles or they're waves. But in the Quantum Reality, some things are Wavicles, both waves and particles at the same time, in potential states, until they become one or the other, depending on how we interact with them.

Because the Spiritual Reality is a purity of Absolutes, the three dimensions that we know in the Material Reality will collapse, just as they do for a photon of light, which has no mass or volume, and the relationship with time will be unique, just as it is for those photons of light.

For example, in this material world we may have a clearly formed Intention to act, then we may perform an action, and the consequences of that action may ramify and reverberate for years or even lifetimes.

In the Spiritual Reality, this relationship changes.

In the Spiritual Reality, the dimensions collapse, joining Intention to Outcome, Cause to Effect and Means to Ends, among other connections.

In the Spiritual Reality, the Intention *is* the Outcome, the Cause *is* the Effect, and the Means *is* the End.

This is why no one can escape the spiritual consequences of their actions: in the Spiritual Reality, it already happened at the instant that they formed the Intention to act. The Intention *is* the Outcome.

There is a saying of Jesus, my favorite thinker: *All they that take the sword, shall perish by the sword*. If we take it to mean that all those who kill others with swords will be killed by sword stroke, we will likely be confused by life, because lots of sword-people live long, happy lives and die by natural causes. But if we think of it in terms of the spiritual logic, it means that the fully formed Intention to draw the sword in violence *is itself the Outcome*, and cannot be escaped.

In effect, Jesus was saying: *No one can escape their karma*. In the logic of the spiritual, the damage of any fully formed Intention has already been done before the sword falls.

From what I've learned, the Spiritual Reality also has its own language, and many words from that language have found their way into Material Reality languages.

Throughout these pages I've capitalized words or concepts that I consider belonging to the Spiritual Reality in order to distinguish them from words belonging to the Material Reality, and to focus my understanding. And I've capitalized the word "Self" because who else is it who offers Devotion, if not the sincere, authentic Self?

Words such as Sacred, Truth, Beauty, Wisdom, Purity, Faith, Serenity, Perfection and Justice, to list a few, are spiritual words, belonging to the spiritual logic system, which is why they are so difficult to define or even explain in the language of the Material Reality. They don't belong to this worldly reality.

The Material Reality version of Justice is fairness, of Beauty it is attractiveness, of Faith it is belief, of Wisdom it is understanding, of Serenity it is tranquility, of Purity it is cleanliness, of Truth it is perception, and of the Sacred it is the precious.

Each of these spiritual language words has a very specific spiritual meaning, which is beyond any of their Material Reality equivalents.

And conflating the two languages, material and spiritual, can result in disappointment.

Justice, for example, is a spiritual concept and rarely attainable in the Material Reality. Perhaps if the department of Justice were called the department of fairness, we might know more clearly what is missing, what to strive for, and how to generate more Material Reality benefits.

Similarly, if Beauty contests were called attractiveness contests, we might see less confusion about what Beauty really is, and why anyone and everyone can be truly beautiful.

Because the Spiritual Reality is non-material and beyond dimensional space and time as we know them, the words of the spiritual language are interchangeable.

To take four spiritual words as examples – Truth, Beauty, Freedom and Wisdom – these are all interchangeable with one another, in any and every combination. However, the Material Reality versions of those words – perception, attractiveness, liberty and understanding – are not.

And the way that we interact with each of the realities, the Quantum, the Material and the Spiritual, is unique to each.

The language of interaction with the Material Reality is motion and forces.

The language of interaction with the Quantum Reality is the exchange of photons of light.

The language of connection with the Spiritual Reality is a sincere, Giving Intention.

In the Spiritual Reality, the Intention is the Outcome, so the focus is on the purity of the Intention.

To borrow a term from particle physics, human-induced Outcomes in the Material Reality are poised in a *superposition state* in the Spiritual Reality, until they are "observed" by an Intention.

In the moment that one has a fully formed Intention to act, the superposition state of probabilities collapses to a single state, called the Outcome, in the Material Reality.

From the perspective of the Spiritual Reality, what we call the "flow of time" is an everlasting now of Intention, a constant "reboot instant" of everything possible.

It means, I think, that spiritually we can be born again with every fully formed Intention. We can't escape the consequences of our actions, but we can wash the stain of the bad we've done from every new decision we make or step we take in life with a sincere, Giving Intention.

By fully formed Intention, I'm referring to those Intentions linked directly to specific actions and Outcomes, not vague, funny, imaginative or nasty thoughts with no direct links to specific actions.

And I learned that the fastest way to clean my own Intentions, when I took my first steps on the Path, was to fill them with spiritual Giving.

SEVA

During my early years in India I had a unique intro-
duction to the concept of *Seva*, or humble service of
a spiritual teacher, church or temple and its grounds.
I watched rich, powerful Westerners scrubbing temple floors, emptying garbage and cleaning latrines,
while surviving on rice and beans. I watched the
Westerners leave the temples and ashrams, giving
their gold watches, chains and rings to the monks
or the Guru's attendants in gratitude. And at some
temples, I went around to the back, and bought the
gold and watches from the hashish-smoking monks
at cutthroat black market prices. Those monks knew
how to haggle, and you can't out-wait them.

So, I was very hard on Seva. I thought of it as a
degrading and demeaning imposition of power. Of
course, that was before I did it.

I get it now. In fact, I understand that a little practice of Seva happens every day before my Devotion, whether I'm aware of it or not.

In the Material Reality, most of us are doing service of some sort for one another, serving in one of a thousand caring categories. In the language of the Spiritual Reality, when such humble service is offered at churches, temples or in the service of a priest or priestess or spiritual teacher, it is known in India as Seva.

Once again, as I see it, religion is what we believe and accept to be true, and the spiritual is what we experience as true.

By this definition, most religious people are spiritual. Yet there are many of us who have no religion but have a deep sense of the spiritual.

Furthermore, I'm referring to a particular form of Devotion here. Seekers on the spiritual Path may engage in many forms of public Devotion, enjoying them and drawing many benefits. I'm only talking here about the intensely private form of Devotion, where we are alone in a connection with the Spiritual Reality.

Alone. In private. This is the kind of Devotion that's done with no audience, no support and no credit. And to engage with that kind of Devotion sincerely, Seva is required.

And the essential lesson to be learned from doing Seva, so far as I can tell, is simply this: humility.

That's it. The tallest wall between where we are now, and any evolved understanding of our Selves, is our pride. I know that from the study of texts and traditions, and from my personal experience.

Thus, the ancient texts on Devotion all insist on some form of humble service as a requirement for all those who seek to walk on the Path. Not to abase one's Self, but rather to purify one's Self of pride and vanity, which are not required for connection with the Spiritual Reality.

When I met a spiritual teacher who practiced extensive penance and sincere Devotion, and put myself at his feet to serve, listen and learn, I noticed after some time that one part of his little temple wasn't as tidy as it could be. I started cleaning up things automatically, and eventually, many months later, I was allowed to clean the Dhuni, or place of sacred fire offerings.

It's worth pointing out that none but a very few were allowed to enter the Dhuni area, and none but a very few would ever risk it. The tradition says that the Dhuni fire is so Sacred that only those with an innocent heart can enter without being burned.

Because I'd seen the burns on people's faces and hands, and their vehement reluctance to enter the Sacred area again, I took the warnings seriously. But

I didn't hesitate and wasn't afraid when I performed the task assigned to me. Not because I'm courageous or spotlessly pure, but because the many months of Seva I'd done had prepared me for that much bigger step in the temple, just as it does for any seeker on the spiritual Path.

I've also found my Seva in removing plastic waste from a beach, caring for stray animals, and simply cleaning up around my own house as a preparation for doing my Devotional practice. Simple, humble service performed with the Intention of serving the Divine Perfection.

What I discovered when I started my Devotion on my own, away from any temple or teacher, was that every day I continue to do some form of unconscious Seva before I begin my two daily Devotions.

This discovery was a surprise: I suddenly realized one day that I never performed my daily Devotion without automatically doing a little Seva first.

As a rational thinker, I can explain this fairly easily. I always wash before doing my Devotion, and I might naturally see a towel that needs to be washed, or a trashcan that needs to be emptied.

But every time? Every single time? No, this was and is the Spiritual Reality, showing me how to perform my Devotion; I've become so used to it that I don't even notice it any more.

And in the years since I did my first sincere service in a temple, I've learned that all active Devotion begins with some form of Seva – with some Giving in the Material Reality before Giving in the spiritual Reality – and nothing prepares you more fully for the first big step on the Path.

ACKNOWLEDGEMENT

It seems ridiculously arrogant for a human being to say, "I Acknowledge You ..." to the Divine Perfection – who are we, to Acknowledge God? – but from everything I've read, learned and experienced, it's required.

And yet, from our tiny, human view, it's no small thing to accept and Acknowledge the existence of the invisible and unknowable Divine Perfection, as arrogant as *that* sounds.

My teacher told me to be innocent.

Be like a kid when you stand before the Divine, he said. *Don't be clever. Don't be mature. How can your maturity or cleverness impress your own Mother, let alone the Divine? Your innocence is all that can connect you.*

Be like a kid, he said, and I did my best.

But it's not that simple.

There's something dizzying and almost frightening about the vast dimensions of space, the solar system, the nearest and furthest stars. Accepting the existence of the Divine Perfection is even more dizzying.

By definition, if there is a Divine Perfection, such a Divinity is ultimately beyond our human-level comprehension. Acknowledgement is a commitment to the ultimately unknowable, and the mind rebels against such a leap.

Moreover, Acknowledgement is a lifetime deal: there's no backing out or trial period. The sincere Acknowledgement of the Divine Perfection is a commitment to the last breath of life. The logic is simple: if there is a Divine Perfection, and if we Acknowledge that, the only sensible response is to make every attempt to connect with that Divine Perfection; and the means of connection is sincere Giving in Devotion. Forever.

Given Acknowledgement, it would be irrational for someone to say: "I know You are there, but I'm busy at the moment, and I'll get back to You."

Sincere Devotion, forever: this is the corollary of Acknowledgement.

To make an analogy, the acknowledgement of the debt we owe to our birth Mother, loving adopting Mother or caring Foster Mother requires Devotion from us in return, whether a particular Mum wanted or needed that Devotion or not. The acknowledgement contains within it the required measure of Devotion, if one is to remain sincere and authentic.

I understood that if I succeeded in opening a connection to a Spiritual Reality, it would become the most significant thing in my life, and that if I wanted to remain authentic and sincere, it would continue for the rest of my life.

And I also knew when making the Acknowledgement that if my attempts at connection with the Spiritual Reality through active Devotion produced no results at all, I would have to be intellectually honest enough to state that.

Sincere Acknowledgement – *I Acknowledge You* – is a required step in every spiritual and theological tradition I've researched. I think the reason for this is free Will.

If we have free Will, and I believe that we do, the logic of Freedom demands that *we are required to make the connection*. If the connection were automatic, or determined by an interfering Divine Perfection, we would not be free, and the concept of free Will would be meaningless.

Because we are free, we must make the first approach – we must be the first to offer Acknowledgement. The Divine Perfection doesn't need the approach, or anything else, because the Divine is beyond wanting or needing: the *connection* requires the approach.

"I know You are there. You know I am here. Thank You for existence, and for this opportunity to Acknowledge You. My daily spiritual Devotion is Yours. I love You, forever."

And having considered all of this for long weeks, after discussing Acknowledgement with my atheist and agnostic friends as often as with my spiritual teacher and other people of Faith, I stood under a rose-violet sky one evening, six years ago, and sincerely Acknowledged the Divine Perfection, as the silvered new moon rose on the horizon.

All that remained before I could begin active Devotion was the next vital step on the Path.

SURRENDER

Spiritual Surrender doesn't mean lying on the ground and being kicked by God.

So far as I can discern, spiritual Surrender means surrendering the elements within the Self that are not required for connection to the Spiritual Reality.

That word – *required* – is perhaps the most significant word in the spiritual language.

Concepts such as good & evil or right & wrong have no relevance in the Spiritual Reality. Those concepts belong to the Material Reality, and have their place in that reality. But the Spiritual Reality, so far as I can tell, is only about what is *required* for connection, and what is *not required* for connection.

For example, we all need a measure of vanity in our lives, or we can end up looking and acting like hobgoblins. But vanity, for all its uses, is not required in the Devotional space of connection.

On the contrary, humility is the key, and is absolutely required.

In the Material Reality we also need a measure of pride to sustain us against injustice and the shocks of modern life. But pride is not required for connection to the Spiritual Reality, and the process of Surrender pushes pride and vanity to the margins of attention during spiritual Devotion.

Once, in the early days of blowing the conch shell in Devotion, I managed a particularly pure, strong note that resounded with astonishing vitality. I thought: *Wow, my teacher would've loved that sound and been proud of me …* It was a moment of pride, a Me-Me-Me moment that intruded on my devotional Giving to something beyond my Self. Over time I've learned to smile when it happens, and then push vanity and pride back into the margins of devotional attention where they belong, until they're required again in the material world.

Vanity and pride are not evil or wrong in the spiritual sense, however problematic their excessive expression may be in the Material Reality, where right and wrong do matter. They're simply not required for connection.

All of the unrequired elements that I've discovered so far, and that I've managed to crowd into the margins of my attention during Devotion, arise in the Ego.

For my purpose, the difference between the Self and the Ego is this: the Self is what admonishes or laughs at the antics of the Ego.

Every enhancement of the authentic Self diminishes the Ego, and every enhancement of the Ego diminishes the authentic Self.

WORTHINESS

Anger, hostility, resentment, jealousy, envy, vanity, pride, malice and fear – none of these are required for connection, and some are serious impediments to connection.

Surrender is the process of making your Self worthy of connection with the Spiritual Reality.

Surrender is an honest Self-appraisal, followed by a sincere process of controlling or eliminating the elements not required for connection, without thinking of them as wrong or evil.

Because the texts and teachers place such strong emphasis on Innocence as the essential gateway to Surrender, the element of *malice* becomes very significant.

Innocence, in the spiritual language, doesn't mean being pure or holy.

Innocence is the benign absence of malice in thought, word or deed.

Cleaning the heart and the mind of any trace of malice or negativity toward anyone or anything, including the Self, is a crucial step in Surrender. In this way a small place of Innocence opens within the Self. It is from this Innocence that we offer our Devotion.

And it doesn't mean that everything is wiped away, and the slate is clean or that we suddenly think we're fabulous. The consequences of our actions go on in the Material Reality for a very long time.

From the perspective of the Spiritual Reality it means that one has a clear understanding of the harm done, authentic remorse, and the sincere Intention not to repeat the harm.

You can't change history, but in the Spiritual Reality, all the things we think of as moments in the constant flow of time are the same: every instant is a new beginning, in its potential for a Giving Intention to determine a Giving Outcome, or the contrary.

My few years of active Devotion have made it clear to me that when travelers on the Path want to see where they are in a given situation, there are two spiritual questions.

1) Am I worthy?
2) How much Giving is in my Intention?

As an example, if I suppose that I've come to know a colleague fairly well, and I would like to take that relationship to a new level of friendship, when looking at it from the perspective of the Spiritual Reality, I should first ask my Self the two spiritual questions.

Am I worthy? Am I worthy of this new level of friendship? Am I in it for the long run, or just for a while? If that person became ill or had a debilitating accident, would I be prepared to help with care? What is my track record with friends? Am I worthy of friendship with this person?

How much Giving is in my Intention? How much of this is about what I can give to this person, and how much is about what I can get?

Similarly, with a stroke of good fortune we may ask ourselves: Am I worthy of this good fortune? Do I truly deserve it? Will I be responsible with this benefit?

And how much Giving is in my Intention, now that I have this good fortune?

When calamity strikes, the two spiritual questions still apply: Am I worthy of this crisis? Can I rise to it with courage? Can I make some preparations to help my Self and others? Is my Faith in my Self, others and the Divine Perfection strong enough? Am I ready to keep contact with family, friends and colleagues through this hardship and be a positive inspiration?

And how much Giving is in my Intention, during this crisis?

Asking my Self these two questions before doing anything new or facing any challenge has evolved as an instinctive practice, and I never proceed until I can answer them satisfactorily.

SUBMISSION

When resentments or envies, unnecessary desires or foolish pride and other unrequired elements in the Self have been tamed to the shadows, the next step in spiritual Surrender is Submission.

Like Surrender, the word *Submission* quite often has a bad reputation. It's often associated with weakness and defeat in the language of the Material Reality.

But spiritual Submission is actually a conscious *admission* of the inescapability of the logic: if there is a Divine Perfection, and if you know it, the only logical course of action is to offer sincere Devotion in an attempt to connect with that Divine Perfection in any way possible, however tangentially.

This is what spiritual Submission means: *You exist, therefore I make every attempt to connect with You, even if my only connection, ever, is through the Spiritual Reality.*

It's the recognition of our own minute insignificance in the great scheme of things, and of the incomprehensible immensity of the Divine Perfection. It's the Acknowledgement of this impossibly vast disparity, and the humility to bend the knees and bow before that Truth.

Submission is acceptance of Truth.

Spiritual Submission is not weakness: it's humility.

The very first little humility and struggle for a place of Innocence that I opened in my heart through that Self-searching process has evolved over time, in a constantly developing relationship with the Path. Yet that little strand of humility I managed to find is itself a form of love – *Look at this world, this Universe! You are magnificent. How could I not love You and serve You forever with my Devotion? How can I not?* – and simplistic as it may sound, it's still the well-spring of every Devotional ritual that I perform, every day. Love.

Spiritual Surrender – the elimination of all in the Self that is not required for connection, and the Submission to service of the Divine – came slowly for me.

There's a lot in my life that I'm ashamed of and deeply regret. Surrender is Soul-searching as well as Self-searching, and for many weeks after I began on the Path, I struggled to feel worthy of the connection to the Spiritual Reality, should such a thing exist.

I definitely had a clear understanding of the harm I'd done in my life, I was deeply remorseful, and for many years I'd followed the sincere Intention not to repeat the harm. But I still didn't feel "clean" enough.

Then one day my Mother said something that changed everything. She put her hand on my head, out of the blue, and said: "You're a good man, my son. You're a good man."

I don't know why Mum said it on that day when my thoughts were troubling me so much, but I took it as a sign that I'd Surrendered, and it was acceptable for me to continue on the Path and take the next step.

RENUNCIATION

I'd been through Surrender, Submission, Worthiness and Seva, and I was ready for the final aspect of Devotion that I had to address: Renunciation.

It's no accident that every ascetic tradition I've studied involves some form of Renunciation. I've discussed this with scholars and spiritual teachers, and it seems to me that Renunciation has two purposes.

The first is to demonstrate – to your Self, if to no one else – that you're committed. In a metaphorical sense, it's like starting a new venture with a gesture of good Faith. The act of renouncing something you particularly enjoy is an act of Giving, offered to the Divine Perfection, in the form of Self-denial.

Obviously, the Divine Perfection is by definition beyond wanting or needing anything that we "give" in Renunciation. But we are free, we have free Will, and in order to establish and enhance a connection to the Spiritual Reality we can freely choose to give Devotion or not to give it.

Renunciation is also required because the Devotee will be performing strenuous rituals, and because the spiritual Path is for life, so every seeker needs the strength to continue through many distractions, and not give up the journey.

It has long been known that encouraging children to delay their gratification is one of the strongest indicators of independent and prudent judgment when those children become adults. Renunciation is the ultimate form of delayed gratification, because it renounces something, many things, forever.

So, I didn't take this lightly.

The Christian traditions have Lenten festivals, where believers forego pleasures and delights, believers in the Jewish tradition endure fasting on Yom Kippur, ten days after Rosh Hashanah, Muslims have the arduous Ramadan observations, many Hindus forego treats and specific foods during certain festivals or on days of the week for life, and similar traditions exist in all the beliefs and religions I've come to experience. Renunciation is there for a reason, and that's to ante up, and to get tough enough to walk the spiritual Path.

Another reason for Renunciation is to minimize distractions from connection with the Spiritual Reality. When seekers have walked a sufficient distance on the spiritual Path, they quite often withdraw from some of their previous day-to-day interactions with the world, not because they abhor the world: on the contrary, because the delights and happy pleasures of the world are very distracting.

In the vocabulary of the Spiritual Reality, Renunciation is the slow and evolving process of winnowing away all in the Self that is not required for spiritual connection.

So, I put some thought into it, and figured out my own version of Renunciation. Among other things, I renounced motorcycles, because I like motorcycles more than just about any other material thing; alcohol; games; parties and some of the things I had collected for years, such as guitars.

My experience tells me that the choices in Renunciation are always personal. It was not required for me to declare to anyone else what I renounced.

And of course, in the Spiritual Reality everything already happened, the second that I had the fully formed Intention to act and renounce.

Acknowledgement, Surrender, Submission, Seva and Renunciation: my studies and experience suggest that these are the spiritual preparations and defenses for those who seek to connect and walk consciously on the Path. They are like the *katas* in Aikido: essential to the fluid evolution of the spiritual art that is being practiced.

Once achieved, these steps lead to the safe, sincere and authentic act of focused, Selfless Giving.

DEVOTION

The big question about spiritual Devotion, which encompasses where, how and when, is why: why offer Devotion to a Divine Perfection that, by definition, is beyond wanting or needing our Devotion, or anything at all?

Teachers and texts differ widely in answering this question. Those that believe in a personal God hold a certain transactional relationship to be in place – you ask God for help, and God responds.

I've seen too many miracles to discount this long-established tradition of asking the Divine Perfection to intervene.

But it has always seemed to me that such appeals for Divine intervention, if one makes them at all, should be reserved for emergencies, and not a part of regular, daily Devotional practice. If there *is* a Divine Perfection, then we're duty-bound to do all that we can within *our own powers* to be healthy, housed, fed and in a position to serve in Devotion with full vitality. We don't ask the Divine Perfection to cut our fingernails.

And it seems to me that in *asking for something* from the Divine Perfection we are on a different frequency of connection, so to speak. In a Universe predicated on the perfect Giving of the Divine Perfection, the logical frequency of connection is Giving, not taking.

When we give our life energy, our innocent essence, in Devotional practice, and we don't ask for anything in return, we are in a state of Selflessness called Grace.

My spiritual teacher told me that one of the purposes of Devotion is to make the Self so clean inside that a tiny element of Divine energy can flow into it. However, bearing in mind that my teacher has been in active Devotion for forty years, and I've only done it for five years, I did not experience any flow of Divine energy.

What I did experience was an undeniable connection to the Spiritual Reality, constantly validated by significant Affirmations and Manifestations.

Knowing that now, for me the purpose of active Devotion is to establish and maintain an ever more profound connection to the Spiritual Reality. It is its own reason for being.

That in turn prompts another question: why be connected to the Spiritual Reality, assuming that such a thing exists, and that it's possible to forge and enhance the connection? Why do it?

The first answer is, *because we can,* and that's not as flippant as it sounds. If there is such a thing as a Divine Perfection, and if it's possible to connect indirectly through the Spiritual Reality, the logic would be to do so.

The second answer is that we are an exploring species, an inquisitive, thinking species, and the spiritual is unexplored terrain for many of us. And as with any exploration of the unknown, there is knowledge to be gained, and there are lessons to be learned.

The third answer is to evolve, and expand the inner horizon of the spiritual Self.

Active spiritual Devotion is its own instruction.

Doing it teaches you how to do it in ever more refined ways. Doing it gives you all the instruction you need to go on, and to go deeper.

And all the while, the spiritual Self is growing and evolving to fill the spiritual space within.

As a fourth reason to do active Devotion, I offer that it's the most energizing, exciting, exhilarating, fulfilling and extraordinary personal experience of my life, and I'm guessing that it's the same for all those who experience the elation of connection with the Spiritual Reality. There is literally nothing like it in this world.

MANIFESTATION

The first years of my active Devotion, particularly the fourth year, were so defined by the phenomenon known as Manifestation, that I should spend some time on it as a final word on my logic system. My notes on this phenomenon when I began my active Devotion show my method or way of thinking more clearly than any explanation.

So far as I can tell, the Path manifests the Path. Walking the Path manifests the Path we walk.

I knew a very nice, aspiring Indian entrepreneur who covered the walls of his studio apartment, including the bathroom, with pictures of a red sports car, always the same model, because he'd been told that he'd get whatever he wanted, which was a red sports car in that model, if he *manifested* it by focusing all of his mental and spiritual power on already having it.

He pasted pictures of himself beside some of the cars, making them look as natural as possible, to imagine himself as already owning the car. He pasted his initials and lucky number over the license plate in every picture. And he looked at those pictures day and night for years.

He drives a family hybrid now, and boasts about its green credentials and its capacity to carry his wife, three children and rescue dog on regular holiday trips comfortably, economically and ecologically. He works in the tech industry remotely from his home office and has what he calls a dream job.

I'll add other elements to the story.

For all those young years while he was attempting to manifest his red car, and finally moving to a new place with no pictures of cars on the walls, and falling in love, and diligently completing his studies, he also did humble Seva service at his local temple, cleaning and cooking and helping with decorations whenever he had free time. He was also devoted to his wife and children, and to his elderly Mother, and took the family responsibility for scrupulous observation of his Mother's last rites, when she passed away soon after the birth of his third child.

The last time we spoke, he said: *I'm very fortunate. My wife loves me very much, and my children respect me and are healthy and well provided for. I'm so fortunate.*

His mental focus didn't manifest the red car, because he never owned a sports car or came close, despite all his wishing for it, but his Devotion *did* manifest *his beautiful life.*

I don't think we can "conjure up" things in our lives just by wanting them. I don't think anyone can *manifest* something from nothing.

I've been in the presence of several mystics who claimed to have such a power, but they were all hoaxers. It took very careful observations to determine that, because they were good at their tricks, but there was always a trick, and I always found it (thank you, magician friends).

What's more, I don't think that anyone can alter the course of future events with their minds alone.

From my study and experience, I think the thing called Manifestation is actually the product of Intention, which is *already and itself* the Outcome in the Spiritual Reality.

In the Spiritual Reality, Cause is Effect and Intention is Outcome. In the language of the spiritual, a worthy Intention *becomes* a worthy Outcome, immediately in the moment of the fully formed Intention to act.

In that sense, the Intention can be said to *manifest* the pathway of the Outcome.

Our Intentions manifest specific pathways, each one an alternate future. Each pathway, in turn, will reinforce the Intention that manifested it. A largely negative Intention will manifest a largely negative pathway, which will tend to reinforce the negative Intention cycle. A positive Intention will manifest a positive pathway, which will tend to reinforce the positive Intention cycle.

Another aspect, from the spiritual perspective, is the *requirement* for a red sports car: the car was not required for his Path, but his highly paid job in the tech industry *was* required to help him meet his valid obligations and responsibilities.

It's conceivable that if he'd abandoned his Devotion, and his family, he might have followed a pathway that led to having that red car, but at the cost of everything else that was precious in his life.

This, in my view, is the phenomenon known as Manifestation. I think this is why some people actually do get things they sincerely and validly desire, and why the texts and teachers constantly remind seekers on the spiritual Path to focus on the pure state of our Intentions, because those Intentions manifest the Path itself.

The trick, so to speak, is to purify the Intention by filling it with spiritual Giving, and then be aware of the opportunities for connection that the Intention-Path synergies continuously manifest in everyday life.

There's a saying: *When the student is ready, the teacher appears*. We might also say that when the Intention is ready, the pathway appears.

I think the positive, Giving, Grace-state of the seeker manifests a pathway of further Devotion, constantly bringing the seeker into contact with all that's required for deeper and more refined commitment, whether that be idols, teachers or wild places to perform rituals. But then the Path gives back, so to speak, in the inspiration to make slight alterations to practice, and to take slightly branching pathways leading to new insights. And with the new insights the seeker manifests the gradually refined practices of the Path, which in turn leads the seeker to more branching pathways.

Each fully formed Intention manifests as a spiritual Outcome, immediately, forming the pathways that we walk on in daily life.

Just as Devotion is its own instruction, walking the Path manifests the Path.

ACTIVE DEVOTION

The two big traditions in spiritual texts are the meditational and the tantric.

There are traditions where monks and nuns live their lives in cells or caves, in solitary contemplation, reciting prayers and mantras. This is meditational, and traditions state that it's very effective at establishing a connection, among other beneficial outcomes.

Other expressions of Devotion require physical actions from the devotee, and these are tantric.

In Islam, for example, worshippers bend at the waist, bow, kneel, touch their heads close to the ground, stand, kneel and stand again, among other actions. This is physical, tantric, active devotional practice, like Yoga. Similar physical movements and actions exist in the Jewish, Christian and Hindu traditions.

My focus has been on tantric Devotion: active, physical and strenuous, by blowing the conch shell.

The conch, being a shell from the sea, produces a completely natural sound: a sound from Nature. It's a soft wail, a siren sound that is sometimes somber and sometimes electrifyingly uplifting. To this day, the Coast Guard authorities in some U.S. States recognize the conch shell as a distress signal, something that occurred to me ironically when I began to blow the conch in Devotion.

In the Hindu tradition, the conch is Sacred. It is both a symbol of auspicious Purity, being closely related to the Goddess of prosperity, LaxmiDevi, and a means of connection at the same time.

I'm not a Hindu, but when my teacher gave me one of his conch shells after three years of study with him, watching him blow the conch hundreds of times in extremely exacting rituals, I knew instantly that I, too, would blow the conch in an attempt to connect – something I had never considered until the conch was actually in my hand.

What I needed to begin, after Acknowledgement, Surrender, Submission and the sincere desire to give in active Devotion, was a focus.

THE SACRED SPACE

I can't adequately express how important it was for me to have a Sacred space for Devotion in my home, but it's also true that the space I started with changed and evolved over time, and now my greatest pleasure in active Devotion is to blow the conch in wild places and under a wide sky of stars, where the devotional space is Nature herself. But I could not have begun in the wild: I needed the discipline of practicing my Devotion in private for three years, before I ventured out.

I've seen Sacred spaces for Devotion made with myrtle branches and seashells, with collage paintings and velvet curtains, with idols made of gold and plastic and tin, with images and inspirational messages and mantras in many languages, with photographs of ancestors, with little shrines in taxis, police cars, shops, banks and hospitals, and in the case of a young Indian boy in the slum where I once lived, with a tiny picture of a Bollywood movie star resting against a pebble on a wooden crate, where he lit an incense stick and offered Devotion with immaculate sincerity every day.

My studies and the responses of teachers informed me that my Sacred space should meet certain criteria.

First, it should directly connect me with the Spiritual Reality in some way, which of course means different things to different people. For me, as one example of things not usually considered inspirations toward the Sacred, a picture of my soul mate instantly connects me to spiritual thinking as effectively as any icon or idol.

Taking advice from my spiritual teacher, I accepted an idol from him as a gift, and chose a couple of other idols and images that worked for me.

Once again, that's a very funny thing to say, from the point of view of the Spiritual Reality, and quite hubristic. In the spiritual sense, I didn't choose the idols: the idols and I chose one another as part of a deeper connection to the Spiritual Reality.

Those idols, at that time, were required as aids to my connection, in the spiritual sense, so we encountered one another in an Outcome that had already happened in the Spiritual Reality, with my fully formed Intention to walk on the Path.

It sounds strange or even a little deranged, at first, but the logic of the Spiritual Reality does make its own kind of sense. The idols chose me, and I chose the idols, and both things are true. In the logic of the Material Reality, only one statement is true: I chose the idols. In the logic of the Spiritual Reality, *both* statements are true.

Another important aspect of the Sacred space for Devotional practice is that it should be beautiful, because Beauty is a characteristic of the Spiritual Reality, just as Truth and Freedom and Faith and Creativity are.

The texts and teachers suggest that the Sacred spaces we set up should reflect these characteristics. So, whatever is spiritually beautiful to us, or expresses true spiritual Beauty to us, will be valid.

The spaces around our personal lives reflect our inner Selves. Any personal office, shop, classroom, living room, privately owned car, truck, taxi, or other "personal space" is literally that: the person, reflected in space. If we take a look around us at our personal spaces, we can legitimately ask: what do they tell us about our inner Selves?

Most of the time, for most of us, this happens as a kind of aggregation over time, in one direction or another, and we often don't notice it happening until we become mindful about it, and examine our personal spaces with a critical eye. Anything and everything in those spaces reflects something inside our Selves.

Of course, we can completely change the way the space around us looks from one day to the next. It's always up to us, and no one is in a position to judge the external truth-space of another person.

I've known tidy people who did very little for others, and messy people who did too much for others. I've known attractive spaces in attractive homes owned by attractive people who did ruthless things. I've known humble, shabby spaces where people lived in deep empathy and affectionate co-operation. We can't judge anyone else spiritually. The concept is invalid: spiritual judging is an oxymoron. All we can do is focus on our own personal spaces, especially our Sacred spaces, and see how spiritually worthy they are.

In the Material Reality, most things gravitate between fear and desire.

A state of balance between fear and desire within any person's Self is what we commonly call a "centered" person. Too much fear leads to timidity, and too little fear leads to recklessness. Too much desire leads to obsession, and too little desire leads to apathy. A balance between what we fear and what we desire, where neither one rules the Self, is both the purpose and the result of following the steps on the Path, because that balance is required for connection in Devotion.

In addition, texts and teachers report that the balance and Beauty of the Sacred Devotional space reflects the level of understanding of the person offering Devotion, because the Beauty we create is an offering, or gift, as the appropriate way to start this and any new relationship. The care with which we might select and wrap a gift to present to a loved one or a new and very important contact is an analogue for the care we should take to prepare a small, humble but beautiful place of Devotion.

In the language of the Spiritual Reality, every beautiful thing is natural, and every natural thing is beautiful.

I used this as a general guide when designing my Sacred space, choosing things and materials that were natural rather than artificial where possible, and esthetically and colorfully pleasing.

Because the Devotional practice I intended to perform involved music and the blowing of the conch shell, I needed to make sure that it didn't upset the neighbors when I set up my space. This wasn't just because it's decent behavior to consider others, but also because I knew that if I were thinking about what the neighbors might be thinking about what

I was doing, my concentration and focus would be severely impaired.

I was fortunate in having understanding neighbors and solid common walls, and I established my spiritual space for Devotion in a corner of the room where any faintly transmitted noise would cause the least disturbance, and where I felt the energy to be right. I bought a simple wooden cabinet with wing-doors, decorated it with silks I'd collected in my travels, installed some concealed colored lights and placed it in the corner I'd chosen, ready to house my idols and images, and to begin my Devotion.

INCENSE, BELLS, GONGS & MUSIC

The many questions I've asked about incense and its use or necessity in several religions and cultures burn down to three main points. First, incense is generally seen as an offering to the Divine Perfection in the form of a pleasant fragrance. This is why many people will shake out the fire of lit incense sticks, and not blow them out with their breath, so as not to impair the Purity of the offering.

Secondly, the fragrant scent helps the devotee to keep focus, joining olfactory sense to sight, sound and touch. The incense creates an atmosphere conducive to spiritual thinking and practice by linking the senses in the committed performance of ritual.

Thirdly, in some traditions, the fragrance of incense is purported to chase away demons and negative spirits, because such ethereal beings, it's claimed, despise the fragrance of devotional incense, for unexplained reasons.

All three points also traditionally apply to the use of bells, gongs and other music to accompany Devotion.

From experience, I find that the simple ritual of lighting incense sticks at the beginning of each devotional practice and ringing a bell for half a minute helps to bring my focus to the moment; to be mindful and ready to perform my devotional practice.

When I began to walk consciously on the Path, my spiritual teacher set me a task: *See if for seven days you can remain entirely and mindfully focused each time you select the incense sticks, light them, wait for them to catch, wave them out, and offer the fragrance to the Divine Perfection in seven circles, for the whole of the small time it takes.*

I couldn't do it. Despite all the steps I'd taken on the Path to prepare my Self for active Devotion, I couldn't remain single-mindedly focused for those thirty or so precious seconds. Not even once, at first, let alone for seven days of flawless focus in a row.

Some little idea or distraction got into my head – worry about my Mother's health, concern over paying bills, even just a happy thought about my daughter – and before I knew it I was out of the moment, waving an incense stick quite unthinkingly, just from memory's habit, and completely focused on something else.

These simple tasks associated with the Sacred space, such as lighting an incense stick or playing a particular piece of music or banging a gong or ringing a small bell for a time, are aids to concentration, and in my case were very helpful in the process of allowing my Self to move beyond the cares of this world and enter into a different world of spiritual connection.

THE IDOL

It had to be Maa Kali.

In each life, my spiritual teacher told me, *we give our Devotion to the Deity that chooses us.*

I've always been drawn to the feminine Divine, the Mother.

In the Catholic school I attended, the renegades, rebels and intractables were not permitted in the Sodalities, or prayer societies, of Jesus or Joseph or St. Ignatius, where all the school prefects were prominent: instead, we were sent to the Sodality of the Blessed Virgin, Mother Mary. It says something about my unruly school behavior or my early Devotion to the feminine Divine, that all of my required Devotion in school years was to Mother Mary, but it was also the one place in that school where I felt at home and at peace, and though I didn't realize it then, connected.

Almost forty years ago a Seer told me that the winged Goddess of fertility, loyalty and love, Isis, was watching over me. I didn't really believe it, but for whatever reason, I've spoken Her name in my mind every day since then, and She still has a place reserved in the Devotion space in my home. In one way or another, She has never left me, even to a silver pendant that I never remove.

Travels around and across India brought me to beautiful temples devoted to the masculine Divine in the form of Lords Shiva, Krishna, Ganesha and Vishnu. I was entranced by the intricate and sometimes opulent temple designs, and admiringly witnessed the Devotion of those attending them.

But the only holy places that held me for any time and drew me back for subsequent visits were those devoted to the Goddesses: Lakshmi, Saraswati, Durga, Dhumawati and Maa Kali.

In city after city across Europe and Africa I also found my Self sitting in churches devoted to Mother Mary in all Her names: Our Lady of Perpetual Succor, Our Lady of the Assumption, Star of the Sea, Queen of Heaven and Mother of Mercy.

I was leading a wayward life at the time, and sometimes limped into a church of Our Lady, begging for help or forgiveness, before limping to a hospital. Despite the reverence and love I felt for

Jesus, I always turned to His Mother when I was in peak distress.

And then there was Maa Kali: a constant presence in my life, through images sent to me by friends and even strangers, references in obscure texts, album covers, the name of a friend's daughter and a hundred other shadow signals.

Eight years ago I walked into the strangest and most unusual Maa Kali temple in the world. I felt an instant connection to the man who became my spiritual teacher and to the idols of Maa Kali, although I was still largely ignorant of the Goddess, and had no idea then what I was letting myself in for, in that first little Surrender.

I was drawn to the teacher at first, and it took me a while to realize that behind the teacher was another energy, another spiritual connection that was drawing me to a convergence of place, teacher, message and Deity that would, for the first time, make sense of it all.

That was the beginning of my instruction in active Devotion, by watching my teacher perform his Devotion, and the beginning (from my ignorant point of view) of my connection to Maa Kali, known simply as Maa. And because of everything that ever happened in my life, it had to be Maa.

Very few people give their Devotion to Maa, in comparison to the vast numbers, the hundreds of millions, devoted to other Gods and Goddesses. Very few idol shops display idols of Maa Kali, amidst the profusion of idols for all of the other Deities.

The reason is that Maa Kali is not a household Goddess, meaning that She is reputed to be dangerous. The legends say that one can offer Devotion to many Gods and Goddesses, and go out into the world and be unscrupulous, and then give more Devotion, and the Deities will forgive you.

But Maa will not forgive. She is reputed to punish hypocrisy and insincerity with scythe and fire.

Whatever anyone may think of this, it's clear that hundreds of millions of Hindus take this seriously, and thus there are few devotees of Maa.

For my part, I cannot accept the logic of a punishing or destroying Divine Perfection, but I do believe that we Manifest the spiritual Path that we walk on in life.

I also believe that if Maa represents the Great Mother-Of-All, then insulting Maa with insincere Devotion is like insulting every Mother in the world at the same time. And in the Material Reality we live in and call the real world, there is little that can match the protection of a Mother's Blessing, and there is little escape from a Mother's curse.

I thought and felt it best not to mess with Motherhood, and to pay supreme respect to the warnings, although I didn't accept the logic of a harmful or punishing Divine Perfection in any form.

And, in fact, the fierce cautions about the terrible consequences of insincerely approaching Maa with Devotion appealed to me.

The inspirational pep talk for devotees of Maa runs like this:

> If you can't do it,
> Tell me you're defeated,
> And leave.

That's just my kind of spiritual challenge.

And I knew that once I started with Maa, if I managed to persevere without being chopped or burned, the Devotion would continue forever.

Defeated, or connected forever.

I loved it. The lack of compromise or an easy way out, the total commitment, the rigid discipline, the lifetime deal and the fearsome reputation of the Goddess were irresistible to me. Several chapters in my life had prepared me for such an uncompromising dedication of my Self to such an uncompromising Deity.

Perhaps I was seeking redemption, a kind of absolution granted by offering my Devotion to Maa and risking fire or sword and surviving … if indeed I did.

But that was at the beginning of my journey on the Path, and I wasn't as sure as I am now that redemption and absolution are Material Reality concepts and in no way related to the spiritual, which is all about what's required to be connected, or not required.

Whatever my deeper motives, I knew in my heart that if I were to acknowledge, surrender and give all of my Devotion to a Deity for the rest of my life, it would have to be from the Goddesses of the feminine Divine, where instinct had always drawn me, and it would have to be the most fearsome, dangerous and beautiful Goddess of them all, Maa Kali.

As it happened, the first idol that came into my hands, given to me by my spiritual teacher, wasn't the terrifying form of Maa but the most gentle and loving of Her many forms, called the Virgin Maa.

She wears a high crown, Her calf-length hair frames a beautiful face, She wears a necklace of skulls on Her bare chest and a battle-skirt, She carries a chopper, a trident and a bowl of plenty, and Her fourth hand is raised in blessing.

I'm writing about this quite matter-of-factly now, but it was a big thing at the time for me to begin my Devotion with an idol. I came from a background that inconsiderately derided idols and idol worship.

The term "idol worship" is inaccurate. Devotees do not worship idols, no matter how much they may revere and cherish them. Idols are gateways to connection and, in theory, the more energy we put through them in the form of Devotion, the more the gateway to connection opens for us.

Friends in Islam and Judaism assure me that idols are not required for them to attain sincere devotional focus. I understand their point of view and agree with it, having blown the conch shell in wild places with nothing but sky, sea, river and tree, but it helped me enormously, at the very beginning of my active, practical Devotion, to have an idol in front of me.

The idols are means to an end, my spiritual teacher told me as he handed me my first idol. *They are not ends in themselves. Your ultimate task is to move beyond idols, prayers, mantras and other devices to a pure and direct communication with the Divine that is a constant, loving conversation from your heart.*

I scrubbed and polished the brass idol of the Virgin Maa until it gleamed, and placed it on a small pedestal on an eye-level shelf in the cabinet, with the red lights I'd installed leaving a soft glow.

I put a few other things in there: a stone that a child had given me; a shell from an Australian seacoast and one from an Indian seacoast; a raw amethyst that my daughter gave me; a glass rectangle with the Maa Kali Yantra, or Sacred design, etched on it; a small brass statue of Lord Ganesha as well as a very small Ganesha that a friend had given me; and a free-standing oval stone from the desert in Australia representing Lord Shiva.

I was respecting the masculine Divine, while Giving all of my Devotion to the feminine Divine in the form of Maa.

My spiritual teacher allowed no compromise in the extravagant beauty of his floral decorations, whenever he performed his rituals. In my Sacred space I arranged tiny bouquets of flowers here and there, until the idol of the Virgin Maa was gleaming within a luxurious pillow of blooms.

I was also following instinct and intuition. Of course, the rituals of Devotion to Maa and Lord Ganesha and Lord Shiva have been articulated for thousands of years by Hindus, and of course I was ignorant, and doing things unknowingly.

But my spiritual teacher had constantly assured me that although the scrupulous attention to the rituals was vital for Brahmin tantric practitioners such as he, they were not required for simple devotees like my Self to make a connection to the spiritual.

No one in the world is a master of the spiritual, he said to me once. *Everyone is learning, and the spiritual is always bigger than any person who tries to master it. Be natural, be simple, be like a kid, be innocent and follow your heart into your Devotion.*

He also said: *Look at me, putting beautiful clothes and jewels on my idols. I'm just like a kid, playing dress-ups with dolls. But unless you become like a kid, you can't open your Self to the Divine. The altar boy is often closer to the Divine than the priest.*

THE FIRST TIME

Bathed, dressed in new, clean clothes and barefoot before my devotional space, I focused the core of my body and my will on what I was seeking to achieve: connection, through spiritual Giving, or at least to satisfy my searching mind and heart, one way or the other.

The music I'd chosen was thumping out a rhythm from the speakers beside me to help me focus, to give me a beat to blow the conch by, to mask the sounds from the streets beyond and to blend with the sound of the conch.

Smoke from blood-red *kumkum* incense whirled and swirled in widening vortices, filling the air with the heady scent.

Because a gentle tradition says that every ceremony or new enterprise should start with recognition of Lord Ganesha, and this was definitely a new spiritual enterprise for me, and since my devotional practice had to start somewhere, for the first blow of the conch I looked at the small idol of Lord Ganesha, using it as a gateway to pure focus.

I was alone in my place, the phone was off and I knew that no one would knock at the door. The room was completely still around me, and seemed to be humming with my Intention.

My eyes glanced left and right. Without realizing the significance at the time, I'd placed a row of pictures of Mother Mary among other redecorations in a corridor weeks before, at exactly the point where my eyes now struck them on the left. My eyes turned right toward a frame of paper butterflies and a Sacred image I'd fixed to the wall on that side, without thinking then that the view left and right of my Sacred space was vitally important.

Everywhere I looked, there was a reminder of what I was there to do, and I hadn't consciously put things and posters together that way. It was one of the first insights of Devotional practice, and I hadn't even begun.

My spiritual teacher almost always blew the conch seven times in a row, in every ritual or ceremony, and I'd decided to follow that example. I focused again on the small idol of Lord Ganesha. I counted out the beat of the song in my mind, preparing my Self to begin. My heart was pounding, but I wasn't afraid. I know fear, and it wasn't that: it was scary excitement, like the moments before you make your first ripcord parachute jump. You're not afraid in those moments: you worked hard to get there, and you're exhilarated beyond fear.

I took a long breath in a steady stream through my nose, trying to push the breath to the bottom of my solar plexus with my mind, wishing that cushion of air down through layers of stomach muscles, deeper and deeper. I raised the conch shell to my lips, and blew out the longest note that I could.

For You, Lord Ganesha … For You … For You … For You … For You …

My skin tightened all over my body as soon as I began. If you've ever been suddenly very afraid, you may know the feeling that your skin is somehow tightening or stretching; even the skin around your eyes. It was something like that.

I had goose bumps on my goose bumps. My short hair was standing up on my scalp. My heart rate accelerated much faster than it had ever done during practice sessions with the conch shell.

I felt strange pinches and aches in my body, and unconsciously adjusted my posture minutely while blowing the conch, standing up straighter until the aching stopped.

And within a few seconds, the strangest and most comfortingly profound *assurance*, something much more than simple reassurance, began filling my mind. It was a deeply intimate feeling that what I was doing was ... *acceptable,* and completely in order, somehow. It was okay.

It's only a personal feeling, but it seemed to me in that profound sensation of assurance that the Spiritual Reality said: *Hi, what took you so long?*

Six bars of the tune I'd chosen was twenty seconds, so I held the note for six bars, and stopped, gasping for breath with a heaving chest and a racing heart.

The music played on. The incense swirled. I regained my breath, counting out a reasonable pause in the bars of music. I was surprised at how labored my breathing was.

When I readied my Self to blow the conch for the second time, I gave respect to Lord Shiva.

I raised the conch to my lips, waiting for the exact moment to begin on the beat, and filled my mind with a Giving mantra:

For You, Lord Shiva ... For You ... For You ...

I blew the conch more confidently than the first time, but the sound was thin and scratchy here and there.

My heart was thumping on a bass drum, filling my chest alarmingly. I've played a lot of sport, but for the first time in my life I felt my heart to be under critical stress, as if the muscles and valves might suddenly lose the rhythm and crash to an erratic stop.

A phrase floated through my mind: *Have Faith … Have Faith …*

I held the wobbling, scratchy note as well as I could. My right knee began to tremble, and I felt a slight jolt in my lower spine. A growing sensation of warmth in my groin had slowly spread outwards as I played the conch until it reached my knees, and then travelled upward to my chest.

My lower back began to shake back and forth and I twisted my body to the left side a little as I drew the very last from the cushion of breath and blew it out in the strongest note I could muster at the full twenty seconds, and then stopped, gasping and exhausted again, my chest heaving as desperately as if I'd completed a sprint race.

Performing the Devotion was much more strenuous than blowing the conch shell in even the longest practice sessions. Just two blows into the sincere set of seven, I was feeling the extreme exertion, and began to wonder if I could complete the set with the same intensity, or at all.

The only real analogy I have is the comparison between training in the gym to be fit enough for six rounds of boxing, and actually *doing* three rounds in the ring. Three rounds against an opponent is more exhausting than six and more in the gym.

I was out of the gym, and in the ring, and puffing hard.

For the third blow of the conch, I'd chosen to focus on the ancient Maa Kali Yantra design, because it called to me very strongly from the first moment that I saw it.

I stared at the design, working to empty my mind and heart of anything but a fully conscious desire to Give the performance of the third conch blow to the Divine Perfection, expressed as the Mothering-Womb-Of-All, beyond names and faces and idols. Maa.

The music pumped around me, just below the volume level of the conch. I inhaled deeply through my nose, pushing the breath down as far as I could into my solar plexus, imagining the breath of air as an amethyst cloud of Giving Intention in my lungs, and compressing the cloud of air to give me the longest and purest blowing of a constant note. I raised the shell to my lips, filled my thoughts with the mantra, *For You … Maa … Maa … Maa …* and blew as powerfully as I could.

An extremely warm, reassuring feeling immediately swept through my mind. It was intoxicating: I wanted that feeling to continue. And then I remembered what I was doing. It was the first time I'd completely lost focus, and had thought about getting something back for *Me*: that lovely warm sensation. It was only the third conch of seven, and I was already thinking about my Self. But that thrilling sensation was so powerful, so wondrous.

I stared at the Yantra design again as I held the note, and then allowed my eyes to drift upward to the light and shadows on the ceiling. My heart immediately crashed into a frantic thumping in my chest as the note of the conch shell sounded out powerfully and clearly for the first time.

I felt the rush of blood through the subsurface of my skin in the exertion. The skin all over my body thrilled with the unusual sudden flow of blood, something like the feeling after supersets in a gym workout.

And for the first time I felt the "head-rush" caused by taking, holding and slowly expelling such deep breaths. Then I realized that I'd closed my eyes unconsciously at some point, and had lost focus on the ceiling.

I've had plenty of rushes in the past and I knew that if I succumbed to the head rush I'd fall unconscious. I opened my eyes, stared at a fixed point of light above me, and pressed my feet as hard as I could against the carpet, grounding myself.

I'm talking about seconds, but it seemed to me then that very gradually I felt the strength rise upwards through my legs, holding me in position, as the focus on the point of light shook the dizziness from my mind, providing clarity of purpose again.

I continued the fairly strong and clear conch blow to the end of the twenty seconds.

I struggled to control my gasping breath and heaving chest.

My heart didn't slow, remaining at a heightened rate, but after about forty-five seconds, my breathing was calm enough to consider the next conch.

In the pause, I recalled that sudden rush of serene assurance I'd felt when I'd begun the third conch, which was even then slowly dissolving within me. I made a mental note and then pushed the thought aside to concentrate on the fourth conch.

In my notes, afterwards, I recorded feeling strangely *encouraged* to continue, somehow, and more confident to proceed at that point.

Borrowing from another worldwide tradition that resonated with me personally, I'd decided to link the fourth blow of the conch to the Ancestors. I made a mantra for myself with a few names of deceased loved ones: my Grandmother, my biological father, and six women and men I'd loved. The mantra of their names ended with the phrase: *And all those who've gone before ... And all those who've gone before ...*

I timed my action to the music, took a deep breath, raised the conch to my lips, looked up at the flickering lights on the ceiling, and blew the long breath out in a single, unwavering note.

It was wobbly, here and there, but it was a strong blast.

My heart rattled against my chest again as I blew, and my skin prickled with a tingling sensation like the furry electromagnetic pull of certain fabrics. For a while it seemed as if my hearing was suddenly alert. I heard all the separate strands of sound that blend into the wail of the conch shell. It was a completely new understanding of the variances within the overall sound. The music playing behind me seemed strangely dissonant for a moment.

And then I sensed movement around me, something moving, behind me, close to me, and then standing in one place a few steps back from where I faced my Sacred space.

I didn't shift my gaze from above. It took a titanic effort of Will to keep blowing the conch and not to look around, because the sensation that someone was standing there, behind me, watching me, was as real as any perception I've ever known.

I was scared, and I have some experience with being scared. Even as my logical mind told me that it might be a draft of air causing a shadow or something else, my heart was racing toward a different truth. It took everything I had to keep going, and not look around.

The twenty seconds extended beyond the six bars I was using as a counter. It seemed that I had much more left within me, so I continued. At thirty seconds counted in bars of music I stopped, choking out the final note.

After a few respectful seconds of waiting, I turned quickly to look behind me, certain that someone had come into the apartment and was standing there. No one.

Birds suddenly trilled into song in my small yard, warbling wildly, the sound of it much louder than anything I'd ever heard. It went on for about fifteen seconds as I recovered and gathered my strength for the next conch, then the birds fell silent. A bell sounded somewhere, tolling a single note repeatedly. I counted to seven clangs of the bell and then the sound stopped. I thought ... *There's no church near here, but ... don't think about it now ...*

My thumping heartbeat didn't slow down by the end of the pause, but my breathing eased and I was able to draw a deep breath. I straightened my back instinctively, allowing my lungs more room to expand. The simple act of blowing the conch four times had exhausted me. I suddenly felt the emptiness in my stomach acutely, because I'd fasted since morning for this early evening Devotion, though I hadn't felt hungry at the start.

I felt a trembling in my arms and legs, showing signs of stress and fatigue, as if I'd ridden a bicycle up several hills. And all the while I was trying to stay in the moment as sincerely as possible and take note of everything that was happening.

I'd chosen to devote the fifth, sixth and seventh blows of the conch exclusively to Maa.

I was already feeling the strain, at just four conch blows. For the first time, as I took a breath and raised the conch to my lips, I consciously diminished the strenuous effort, thinking that if I didn't soften the blowing of the conch a little, I wouldn't have sufficient strength to continue to the seventh conch.

I blew the conch more gently, allowing my eyes to drift upwards as I slowly raised my arms to maintain the sustained note. A strange feeling, a little bit like suddenly realizing that you missed your stop on the train, rushed through my mind, filling me with doubt.

The conch note was shaky and burbling. I had to shift the sound-aperture around in my mouth as I blew, constantly searching for a clear note. Even the note I eventually found fluttered weakly, and I barely made it to the twenty seconds.

In the next pause I considered what had happened. I knew that I hadn't been afraid or worried. The feeling was different. It was a little like when you try to screw on a container lid, but the thread hasn't exactly caught: the more you twist, the less it connects and seals.

I'd tried to reserve my energy for the seven blows, but this had diminished my commitment, and the conch blow failed to ignite.

Okay, I thought, responding to my second insight from the Spiritual Reality, *it's total commitment or nothing at all, even if I don't make it to the end.*

I blew the sixth conch with everything I had.

For You ... Maa ... Maa ... Maa ...

Halfway through the twenty seconds of music I felt my head growing light, and I began to sway unsteadily. I realized that my eyes were shut again, but didn't know when I'd shut them. I opened my eyes and stared at a fixed point above me. My sense of balance returned as I continued.

When the six bars for the sixth conch ended and I stopped, my chest stretched to bursting, I felt strangely empowered to continue, and was certain that it would be within my capacity.

And then a sudden piercing emotion ached from within, traveling all the way to my trembling hand, as I realized that only one more blow of the conch remained.

I gave everything, knowing that this was the last conch of my first attempt at connection through sincere Giving Devotion. At ten seconds, the true note on the conch sounded for the first time. I'd never heard that strong, clear, ancient sound in my practice sessions.

I struggled to control my delighted and grateful surprise in order to maintain the pure cadence of the note, keeping my lips tightly pressed to prevent leaks of air, my cheeks filled with a constant supply of breath fed slowly from deep in my solar plexus, and my hands in the precise grip on the conch to maintain the strange new note – a grip I'd never tried before in all my practice sessions.

I lost focus on my mantra. I lost my surroundings. I closed my eyes. I felt the breath, the amethyst cloud, being driven upwards by layer upon layer of muscle, until every last molecule of air was forced out of my body and into the conch. Instead of timing my Devotion to the music, it was as if, for a moment, the music was accompanying me.

And then the music stopped, and I continued with the conch for some time until I faltered, and sounded the end in one blast.

In the silence that followed, I turned off the lights in my Sacred space, staggered to my desk and wrote down my notes while they were still fresh in my current memory.

I look through those notes now, those first observations from the first time, and surprise myself with how clinical I was when I first started to walk on the Path of active Devotional practice.

I began this journey as a scientific rationalist, making the leap of Faith, boldly going where many had gone before, and taking notes along the way, a naïve but reasoning explorer in the spiritual, taking notes for my Self. I didn't understand then that you don't explore the spiritual, the spiritual explores you.

I'm also a little further along the way than I was then, not much, but a little, and I look at how structured I was, and realize that I was coming at the whole "process" mechanically, because I was coming from a paradigm, or way of thinking, that I deeply respected – *the scientific method* – and saw most things through that lens.

I know now that most of the structures that I created for my active Devotional practice changed as

I developed my practices organically. But I also know that the structure I had at the beginning helped to keep me grounded.

It took several minutes for the waves of exhaustion, excitement, bewilderment and awed elation to pass after I performed my first active Devotional practice, and for me to return to what I might now call my *spiritual resting state*. I was simply astounded at the intensity of the undeniable validation I felt I'd experienced. It had worked.

The first notes I took were written in a shaky hand. I tried to define the strangely elated fatigue that I was experiencing afterwards. One total sensation was exhaustion. Another total sensation was elation. It was as if my body was fully aware of the strain, but my mind was excited and working fast, and both things were equally valid.

A large house-spider, a hunter of venomous spiders, stalked on its long, thin legs high across the wall above me, and stopped at a picture of a Sacred fire, taken during a devotional ceremony. The spider swayed in place for some time, doing a spider dance, and then remained still above the center of the picture. For two months, as it turned out.

A rooster crowed in someone's backyard. I looked at the clock: seven and a half minutes had passed, and yet it had seemed much longer. There was a silent stillness around me then, as if everything in the world stopped for an instant, even the clock.

As I thought the word *silence*, the birds suddenly chattered in squeaks and song again, bringing me to the moment. The clock ticked over the beginning of a new minute, and I heard the faint sound of traffic in the street, a hundred meters away, which had always been there, but had somehow vanished for a while.

I was back in the world again, but the experience of blowing the conch was still reverberating within me like the hum of a gong and was as "real" as anything I could touch.

There was a question I'd based my research and sincere Intention on asking: *Does it work?*

The self-evident answer was yes, it did. I knew that to be true within the experience of it. But the rational thinker in me wanted to discard anything that could be explained logically and without reference to the Spiritual Reality.

QUESTION EVERYTHING

Long habits of thought made me question every detail of the experience, but now I had a different lens through which to view what was happening to and around me.

This is another of the blends of rational and spiritual perspectives that make sense to spiritually aware people but seem irrational to my determinedly materialist friends.

To be authentic, a spiritually aware person strives to hold both perspectives, the material and the spiritual, and to give each respect.

When I calmed down enough from my first experience, I went back to basics and questioned everything, but left the spiritual lens over one eye.

I went back through all of the effects I'd noted during the performance of the Devotion, and examined them.

First, there was the sensation of my skin *tight-ening* somehow, with accompanying goose bumps all over my goose bumps, and the sensation that my short hair was standing on end as my scalp tightened and tingled.

I was prepared to dismiss this as manufactured by my own sense of the magnitude of what I was doing, or trying to do. In a sense, I allowed that I was *spooking myself*, so to speak. So, I let that one go.

I know now that I was wrong about that, and in my further experience, at any rate, this sensation only increases in intensity, every time I perform my Devotion. The first conch blow of seven is always *a blast to the system* as my spiritual teacher says. But at the time I was happy to let it go as just an emotional reaction.

The elevated heartbeat seemed easy enough to explain through the exertions involved. Now, however, some steps along the Path of practical Devotion from that starting point, it seems to me that the elevated heartbeat isn't a result of the conch blowing, *it's required to achieve it*.

The sudden pinches of pain and strange aches I'd felt were easily explained as the result of a new level of strenuous effort in blowing the conch: a level far beyond any I'd achieved in practice. My notes say: *new activity, new pinch on a nerve, change your posture to adjust: simple.*

From today's viewpoint, I don't agree with my Self for discarding something so fundamental – the changing shape and posture of a person – so casually. There's a lot more to it. My posture has significantly changed since I began blowing the conch, and that change is ongoing.

The strange sense of assurance and calm, although quite intense, could be explained then as simply a case of action's confidence flowing through me, and replacing anticipation's anxiety. I saw it then as just a feeling of relief, in other words, to actually be started in the practical Devotion I'd been preparing my Self for so long to perform. I was experiencing nothing more than a normal rush of relief, with all of the brain's usual nice-chemical-and-hormone suspects involved.

I don't think so now, more than five years and thousands of times after that first session: I think spiritual assurance is a genuine spiritual charac- teristic, rarely experienced in the Material Reality except through trust-filled love. It's a kind of Truth, a background hum of the Spiritual Reality. Another name for it is Faith, and for the moments of blowing the conch for the Divine, very sincerely, we are Faith-filled.

In the next note I made that first time, I referred to the thin and patchy tone I'd managed on the second conch. I asked my Self a question in the margins: *How pure does your Devotion have to be? Can it be flawed and yet still be valid, if it's sincere?*

I think that I know the answer now: it's not the perfection of the performance that counts; it's the perfection of the commitment to the performance.

Those questions in the margin of my early notes show that from the beginning it concerned me that my devotional practice wasn't … perfect. And of course, it can't be perfect. But it took me a while to stop concerning myself with "perfecting" my performance in Devotional practice.

Every now and then, I'll blow the conch seven times in a row in perfect time to the music, and with powerfully sustained notes each time.

But, so what?

I finally came to understand that it would be possible for someone to blow the conch almost perfectly *in terms of execution*, and yet have less *commitment* than someone else, whose very sincere performance was shaky and flawed. I came to know that some of the shakiest performances I've done were among the most memorable, and provided the most charismatic connection experiences. Those shaky performances forced me to work harder and give more. It's not the almost-perfect practice that counts: it's the almost-perfect commitment to the practice.

The next observation in my notes referred again to that powerful, warm feeling of assurance I'd experienced, when the third conch began. Although the feeling was quite intense, and qualitatively different to other tranquility and contentment experiences I'd known in my life, I was still prepared to dismiss that feeling as a naturally occurring emotional state provoked by the release of certain biochemical compounds in the brain-body matrix.

I knew from research that these compounds induced states of mind. And I knew that these states of mind were sometimes confusing, within our Selves, because we might be entirely unconscious as to the true nature of the chemistry-and-experience provoking them: we might think that one type of experience has occurred, but may in fact be "tricked" by our body's chemistry into thinking and feeling a certain way.

So, I was prepared to dismiss that feeling as just a byproduct of another process, rather than evidence of a mystical or profoundly spiritual connection.

I was wrong: it's much more significant than that. Connection with the Spiritual Reality is a warm safe zone, a refreshing, clean Jamaican river for the soul. But I'd only just started, and I was applying the most rigorous tests that I could to everything I was experiencing, thinking that such a method was valid.

My next note from the third conch refers to losing focus. The feeling of assurance was so strong that I succumbed to its pleasure, and wanted it to continue, and focused on it, losing my pure focus on Giving.

I came back to this point many times in my notes, in early years. Paradoxically, I now realize that the early attention paid to maintaining focus during Devotion is a key to *losing focus appropriately* later, and enhancing the connection. It sounds strange, but in the spiritual sense we discipline our focus in order to successfully abandon it. Refining the focus is also the most difficult aspect of the practice to sustain with Purity.

And I've come to realize that there's always something to learn, even from the stray thoughts that intrude on the pure focus during Devotion.

Rather than flaws in Devotion, they can be revelations. As I've found ways to ease such thoughts into the margins of consideration during Devotion over time, I take note of them as expressions of some important preoccupations in my daily life, a little like lucid spiritual dreams, and try to learn from them.

My third note related to the "head rush" I'd experienced. I was content to put that down to a hyperventilation effect, brought on by holding deep breaths and expelling the air slowly.

I've reconsidered that first easy dismissal of the *head rush* effect, after many hundreds of head rushes. I think now that the head rush is simply a sign of full commitment, and always and only occurs when the focus is intense. It's one of those *get used to it* things, because it isn't going to stop, so far as I can tell.

I may be giving the impression that after blowing the conch in sincere Devotional practice for the first time, I donned a white lab coat and wrote down my notes in a cool, calculated scientific manner. On the contrary, I was extremely excited and elated, and it took me half an hour to calm down completely.

I knew that it had worked, to put it crudely, and I'd had a profound spiritual experience, because I was electrified by it. One sage explained first contact with the spiritual as *A Very Deep Wow*. I was in the Wow.

But I wanted to be ruthless in discarding anything that could be explained away with science or coincidence. I think differently about all that now. It seems to me that the Material Reality explanations and the Spiritual Reality explanations run parallel to one another, and are not in contradiction: they're both true and they're both right, so to speak.

When I blew the fourth conch, for the Ancestors, I noted a wide range of effects and occurrences: my heart rattling against my chest unnaturally, my skin prickling all over, a heightened sense of alertness and hearing, the vivid sense of something moving and then standing behind me, the sudden screeching of the birds when I finished the conch, the tolling of a bell seven times, the emptiness in my stomach, the stretching of my spine, and the sudden onset of fatigue.

I went through each of them, dismissing all but one in turn. The elevated heart rate was normal, after four blows of the conch. The prickling sensation was simply oxygenated blood, caused by the deep breathing and exertion. The birds and the tolling of the bell were dismissed as coincidences: there are no churches nearby, and I've never heard that tolling bell before or since, but some car alarm signals have a tolling sound. My spine straightened because I was stretching to take in more air. And the sudden hunger and fatigue were simply biological responses to the stress and exertion of the practice.

I wrote them all off as non-spiritual or non-meta-physical occurrences then, and of course I've revisited that thinking on each point, because some of these phenomena and others have occurred many times since that first active Devotion.

But the sensation of a presence behind me was too strong to dismiss, no matter how many times I rationalized the event to my Self as nothing more than a "spooky" effect of the practice within my own imagination.

Now I know that this sensation occurs from time to time, as if some entity has come to watch you perform your devotional practice, to put it artistically, and it's always significant.

I've discussed this with my spiritual teacher and consulted the texts, and they agree that this sense of an accompanying presence from time to time during active Devotion is a common spiritual experience.

That *spooky presence* was something I filed away under *metaphysical*, because the experience was too vivid to ignore. In too many years of prison and the wild road, I've learned to tell the difference between the *illusion* that someone is there, and the *reality* that someone is there.

I knew that something strange had happened, and I knew that it was a genuine experience, but I couldn't begin to understand it or even describe it adequately then.

And I don't write off spiders, birds, bells and numbers so easily now: I actually look out for them.

The fifth, sixth and seventh conch blows were exclusively for Maa, which was the focus I'd chosen as my personal connection.

The fifth conch was a crisis of Faith, in a sense, because I held something back, worried that I wouldn't have the strength to complete the Devotion. It was my first big lesson from the Spiritual Reality on the question of commitment, and not the last.

All or nothing.

It doesn't matter if you think you'll fail; just give it everything you've got, each time you do it. And from my experience so far, the Devotion never lets you down. I've never failed to complete a set once I started it, even in the most exhausted state: just starting it, and doing it, always sees me through to the end.

The sixth conch was subsequently much stronger, but during it I felt my Self sliding into unconsciousness. In my notes at the time, I warned against closing my eyes too often during the Devotion, and to be wary of losing consciousness.

Since then, I've passed out completely in one of the most spiritual experiences of my life, and teeter on the edge of unconsciousness at least once in almost every daily Devotional practice. I have a different view of the phenomenon, but my notes from the time wrote the warning in large letters in the margin: DON'T PASS OUT!

A feeling of intense sadness preceded the seventh and last conch, as I realized suddenly that the Devotion would soon be over.

It was a strange sadness. For example, if you imagine that a good friend were taking up a wonderful opportunity in another country, you might feel happy for her, but sad for your Self at the same time. It was that very sweet, innocent kind of sadness.

And then the note from the conch on that last blow was "correct" for the first time, so to speak. I heard a note I'd never heard before. In a sense, it felt as if the Devotional practice itself was teaching me how to blow the conch properly.

I recall being elated that such a new, pure sound had emerged from the conch, and then trying to suppress that elation to focus again on Giving, rather than on the astounding gift of instruction I felt I was receiving.

And then I lost my way, and only came back to the moment when the music stopped, and I blew the conch to the last of my air. Somehow, I'd entered a little "trance state" for about ten seconds.

My eyes were closed, but I "saw" shapes, colored lights and patterns shifting, dissolving and transforming. It was as though I was looking at the world from a strange, side-on angle, where things were familiar but completely different at the same time.

I've discussed this phenomenon many times with my spiritual teacher, because *trancing* in this way has become commonplace during my active Devotion. He described trancing as not just required in devotional practice, but the very purpose of it.

It's in trancing, he said, *that we know the world beyond illusions.*

At the end of my first practical Devotion experience and its early analysis I was ready to dismiss most of the perceived effects as fully explicable in scientific terms, but I was in no doubt that I'd had a mystical journey of connection to the whatever it is that might be called the Spiritual Reality.

And this is where the spiritual and the material stare at one another across a linguistic and conceptual abyss.

The scientific method is predicated on *experimental validation for third parties to observe.*

The spiritual is predicated on *experiential validation for individuals uniquely to experience.*

It's the difference between knowing something as a fact, or information, and knowing it from experience: between knowing that LSD inspires hallucinations as a clinical fact, and actually having the trip your Self. One is a set of facts *out there,* and the other is a set of Truths *in here,* within the Self.

Moreover, in the scientific method you have to *duplicate it* experimentally for others, in order to "know" it verifiably.

In the spiritual, you have to *experience it uniquely* for your Self, in order to "know" it verifiably, and you can repeat the experience for your Self, but not duplicate it: it's unique each time.

This is the river between science and the spiritual, I think, and one of the reasons why it's so difficult to articulate the spiritual to the satisfaction of a scientist or a rationalist philosopher, and vice versa: one is experiment and the other is experience.

The scientific method proceeds from the proposition that there are fundamental laws in the natural world that can be discerned by observation and experiment.

I proceeded from the assumption that if there is such a thing as a Spiritual Reality, that there must be fundamental "laws" or rules of logic that apply to that meta-physical Spiritual Reality, and that connection to the Spiritual Reality was possible for anyone, anywhere, through authentic, sincere Giving in active, physical devotional practice.

I codified my observations during the devotional practice, and have continued to do so for more than five years now. But no matter how meticulous my notes, no matter how precise my observations, the spiritual experience remains individual, and virtually impossible to convey adequately to another mind.

After my first active, practical Devotion, I was ready to dismiss most of the observable effects as explicable or coincidental, and only two things remained: the sense of a presence behind me, and the ten-second trance state during which I'd lost my usual contact with the Material Reality, and entered another Reality.

Knowing the difference between *merely thinking* that something or someone is behind you, and there *actually being* something or someone behind you, has saved my life several times. The feeling I experienced while blowing the conch was distinguishable from, but almost identical to, every true warning from my instincts in the past, when there really *was* someone there, with a knife or a gun or a club.

I *knew*, in that prison sense, that there was someone or something behind me. It took a tremendous effort of Will not to look around during that sensation's compelling vividness.

In itself, *not* looking around was an act of Surrender, and a pure act of Faith, especially when my life experience proves that the consequences of not obeying your instincts are dire. I was spooked, to speak frankly, and I don't spook easily.

I was right not to regard it as a natural phenomenon. It will sound strange to anyone but the seers I've consulted and my spiritual teacher, but when those ... *visitors* ... come to watch me perform my Devotion now, I welcome them. And some are repeat guests.

I know from experience that, just as my teacher assured me, the trance state becomes *most* of the Devotional practice after some time, and that most of the insights come in those long seconds beyond time and space as we know and experience them in the Material Reality.

For my Self, at least, I know that the trance state of emptiness and openness in the midst of Devotional practice is the Giving beyond Giving.

The funny thing to me now is that I did all that thinking and logic and reasoning, trying hard to devote my Self with a scientific method, and then all of it was blown to the moon on the very first conch of the second year.

But that was just the first time, at the start of the long, first year, and I didn't know that all the instruction I would ever need comes from simply doing it.

My notes were cool and clinical, because I was striving for rigorous thinking, but in fact I was thrilled beyond my wildest expectation, both during and after that first attempt, and the thrill has evolved over years into persistent exhilaration.

But a little question curled around like a leaf in the breeze of elation, and I wrote it on the last page of my notes: *Will sincere Devotion work, the second time?*

It did. It always does.

THE FIRST YEAR

The conch is an instrument, like a trumpet, and like any instrument it takes long hours of practice to blow strong, consistent notes every time you try. I was focused on technique very much in the first year, changing the shape that my lips formed, changing the position of the conch shell and modulating my breathing.

Still, the notes I wrote for the ninth month show that the best I could manage at that time was four near-perfect blows of the conch in any one set, with three blows well below the standard I'd set for my Self.

Despite that, I remember feeling more confident in what I was doing with every flawed performance, every day. I approached my Sacred space without apprehension, feeling ready to proceed. I knew that I was connecting, and had no doubt about the process.

It was my own part in it, the poor blowing of the conch, that failed to meet my hopes.

And even though my conscious, mindful attention wavered, causing me irritated distress from time to time, I looked forward to each day's Devotion eagerly, determined to improve my performance.

I changed the music only once that first year. When I found that I could easily accommodate the seven blows in the first tune I'd chosen, I selected a new tune that was as conducive to focus but longer, requiring me to sustain the blows of the conch for twenty-six seconds each time, to match the beat and bars of the tune.

It had taken me four months to match my conch playing to the beginning, middle and end of the first tune, so that the last note of the music coincided with the last second of breath in the conch. The new tune took me just two months, and I stayed with it in the longer breathing regime until the year's end.

The music, bell ringing, candle lighting and incense helped me much in that first year, when I was away from my spiritual teacher and doing my active Devotion alone.

Another sustaining factor was the support and understanding of my soul mate, A.

I don't know if it would be possible to do what I did, to go off the grid, take the leap of Faith and become actively devoted, if my life companion had not engaged with it as supportively as she did. For six years, and counting.

And I was very fortunate to have the constant example of my spiritual teacher, whose sincerity in the performance of his Devotion is without parallel in my experience, and who always responded to my hundreds of questions with patient wisdom.

My Mother and Stepfather were also approving, and encouraged me to continue, when they saw the Path that I was taking.

My grown up children were very grown up about it, and told me to go for it.

My lovingly skeptical brother asked me: "You blow a shell twice a day in front of a brass idol. Tell me, what's crazier than that?"

"Well, how about … how I *used to be*, back in the day?" I replied.

He agreed, and has vitally supported me, because by the end of the first year, many things had already changed or begun to change for the better.

They were subtle, incremental changes that I didn't notice at the time but that added up to a very significant alteration of my personal surroundings.

Framed movie posters I'd put on the walls of different apartments for years came down or fell down, and one by one each empty space was filled with framed pictures of my family and other loved ones and art made by friends.

My decades of riding, repairing and modifying motorcycles had given me quantities of motorcycle paraphernalia and mementoes. Somehow, they all disappeared, given away without me noticing it happening.

I experienced a burst of creativity, making new sculptures and collages, and composing new music. Creative works filled corners and hung on walls.

India had given me a taste for extravagant color, but by the end of the year the colors floated from room to room in floral garlands and banners of silk saris given to me by friends, reflecting sunlight and overhead light in reds, yellows and greens. The whole apartment glowed in haloes of colored light.

The music I bought and listened to was also changing. I look back through the playlists I'd compiled before my Devotion began. There are many songs of rebellion, anger at injustice and some epics of the criminal and outlaw life. I recall the reasons why I chose those songs for my list, but somehow my thinking had changed in that year. However valid I had considered the choices, they seemed irrelevant now.

My current playlists are full of songs about love, and the hope for love, and the determination never to give up, no matter how tough life gets. By the end of the first year, I didn't play any of the rebel songs from my previous lists, and I was listening to new music from new lists.

This may seem like a small thing. For me, it was huge. Music is the first thing in the morning and the last thing at night. I write to music, draw, make collages and sculptures to music, exercise and dance to it every day, and do my active Devotion to music. I also compose music and write songs.

The change to a completely new set of musical inspirations, therefore, was immense, but the strangest thing for me was that I didn't notice it happening until the end of the year. How could something so vital to my happy Creativity change so fundamentally, without me noticing it until it had already happened?

But this occurred in the movies and television series that I chose to watch as well, and in the novels that I chose to read.

I'd always had a fun spot for well-made horror movies, and like many I'd always enjoyed action and crime films. By the end of the year there were no films in those categories in my playlist. Instead, there were dramas about moral or ethical choices people make and their consequences, love against the odds, and some light comedies. It wasn't that I disliked the other movies: if I saw a cleverly made one by chance,

I still kind of enjoyed it. But my subliminal choices were all in a new, different direction.

Because I was off the public life and social network grid, I spent much more time with my family and close loved ones than I had in years.

And this transformation occurred organically, without conscious planning, and it continues to this day.

The first year ended with a sense that I was in a better place within my Self and with my loved ones, a stronger conviction that I should continue, and a determination to improve my performance.

I'm smiling now, going through the solemn notes I made at the first year's end. If only I'd kicked back and enjoyed it more, instead of worrying so much about things that didn't really matter much.

But all of those irritations and frustrations resolved themselves in an instant, when I blew conch for the first time, in the second year.

THE SECOND YEAR

It was the first new moon of the second year, and an auspicious one, my spiritual teacher said, adjuring me to be rigorously disciplined in my sincerity while performing active Devotion at that time.

I'd performed the monthly ritual of cleaning the idols and redecorating the Sacred space, and all was in order. I was bathed and dressed in lightweight, new clothes for the occasion.

As the crescent moon rose over the horizon, I took deep breaths and focused on tidying up my Intention.

Like everyone else, I wanted things. No matter how strenuously I tried to focus exclusively on Giving, I wasn't immune to desire. In my case, what I wanted was deeper understanding, which has always been my drug of choice, and an ongoing connection. I didn't want the active Devotion to stop. Someone once asked my spiritual teacher why he put himself

through such extremely strenuous and painful exertions in the performance of his Devotion. He replied:
To get the strength to do it again, tomorrow.

It seemed important, at the beginning of my
second year, to get what I wanted out in the open,
so that I could ease it aside into the margins of my
attention once I began.

Next, I focused on my loved ones, gently easing
those beloved connections to the sides of concentration, so that worry about them or joyful thoughts of
them might not blur my focus.

I lit the candle, lit the incense sticks, rang my
small temple bell, and then switched on the music,
the same piece that I'd used for the last few months
of the previous year.

I pledged my Self to the task, raised the conch to
my lips and blew for Lord Ganesha, the beginning of
all spiritual rituals.

The blow was a little wobbly, but I sustained it
to the end. The second and third conch blows were
the same. Then I blew for the Ancestors.

I entered a now-familiar trance state, my eyes
closed, forgetting the names of those gone before,
and then an image came into my mind. It was the
face of a young woman, seen as though in a silvered,
gossamer sheen, white on white, and silver on silver.
She was wearing a shawl on the back of her head,
and her hair was free to her shoulders. She wasn't

smiling, but her beautiful, radiant face was utterly serene, as if beyond all care, beyond even love itself. For a moment the face seemed oddly familiar, and yet I knew I'd never seen it before.

Then a name spoke in my mind. It was a voice I didn't recognize, neither female nor male. There was a hush of breathy sound and then a name, pronounced very clearly: *Hush ... Prabha.*

The image dissolved slowly and I felt myself to be tottering and wobbling in place. I was still blowing the conch. The music had passed the point where I should've stopped.

I shook my Self back to the moment, breathing in gasps, my heart beating chaotically in my chest.

The last three conch blows passed without incident, in reasonably strong, fluid tones.

I stumbled to my desk and wrote down all the notes that I could. Then I called my spiritual teacher.

Guruji, is your Mother's name Prabha?

No, it isn't.

Pause.

But ... it must be.

No. That wasn't her name.

But ... Sir ... it ... has to be.

There was another pause. People rarely contradict my spiritual teacher, or would have cause to, which is one of the reasons why I love him.

Oh, he said at last, *you mean her childhood name, which was changed when she was twelve years old. Yes, that was HemaPrabha. But nobody has spoken this name in sixty years. How do you know it?*

It was impossible for me to know it. In all my years in India I'd never heard the name, and no one had ever spoken it in my teacher's ashram. But I *did* know it, and knew it with such certainty that I contradicted my teacher.

It was a profound connection. The conch shell I was blowing had belonged to my spiritual teacher's Mother, and she had blown it every day. For the last ten years of her life she was completely blind, but her daily Devotion with the conch continued until her death.

My spiritual teacher had presided at her Hindu cremation, blowing the same conch shell.

He blew that shell for ten years or so, until some visiting monks from Nepal presented him with new conch shells, and he put his Mother's shell aside for use only on special occasions.

Then he gave it to me. And I started blowing it, all the way across the world.

It may serve to encourage others on the Path who feel that their progress is slow that it took me all of that first year of daily Devotion with the conch to realize that my own Devotion is just a link in a Sacred chain.

My spiritual teacher's Mother was a person of such exquisite Purity in her Devotion that her conch shell is still being blown, oceans away, by a foreigner, someone not raised in the Hindu traditions, and more than twenty years after her passing.

I suddenly understood, with that first session of active Devotion under the rising new moon, that I was blowing the conch for that devoted Lady, as much as for my Self, and I was continuing her sublime Penance with the beginning fragment of my own. And that one day after I'm gone, if I were sincere enough and fortunate enough, someone would blow the same conch shell with sincerity, and continue our Devotion, hers and mine.

I was blowing the conch for her and for my Self at the same time, in a spiritual relationship beyond time.

It was humbling and somehow a little wonderful to think that the big idea of my own Devotion was actually in the service of a prior Devotion that began before I ever took a conscious step on the Path.

I modified my system of seven blows of the conch to make the third conch for her, HemaPrabha, that devoted Lady, saying her name over and over.

And when I blew the conch on the second day of that second year of Devotion, thinking of her, the sound rang true, every time until the seven were complete. The frustrations of the previous year disappeared. Every time I blew the conch I found a clear, strong sound. Sharing my active Devotion with my spiritual teacher's Mother opened the doors to better performance and much closer focus.

From that day to this, no matter how fatigued, ill or injured I may be, that third conch blow for her always gives me the energy to complete my set.

In mid-year, my Mother was informed that the cancer she'd been hoping would stay in remission had flared up, and this time there was no cure. My soul mate and I took an apartment three doors from my Parents, and we joined the family in caring.

My daily Devotion continued, strengthened perhaps by the powerful emotions we all felt at that time, and by my Mother's courage.

At year's end Mum had already outlived the predictions, and with a routine of caring that seemed to be helping Mum to cope, I entered my third year of Devotion in cycles centered on my Parents' needs.

THE THIRD YEAR

I think of the third year as the Year Of Defiance and Affirmation.

Everything was going well. Mum was relatively pain free, Dad's very troubled heart hadn't caused any major alerts, our projects were on track, and my active Devotion was more energetic and focused than ever.

But for some reason, I found my Self disregarding times to perform my conch, omitting sets completely, blowing eight or nine times, and on one occasion sixteen times, and blanking mantras that had been very effective conduits to connection.

I re-read some texts and consulted with my spiritual teacher, and it seems that this phase, which he laughingly called *the cheeky phase*, is very common, and quite important. This defiant stage questions everything, not with doubt or hostility but as a challenge. My teacher assured me that it was a natural reaction and that it would pass.

My experience was that the defiance was a kind of breaking out from the perhaps overly reverential ways that I was going about things. In its way, extreme reverence for *things* and the punctilious observation of ritual is a kind of fear, and the defiant phase chased away the last vestiges of fear.

Unfortunately, the defiant phase is often marked by outbursts of anger. My spiritual teacher warned me about this, but it happened anyway.

By year's end I'd managed to bring the sudden, explosive surges of energy under control. The formula that my teacher gave me was this: *Give your excess energy to your life companion and to the Divine in Devotion. Don't waste such a precious thing.*

Then, on a moonless, star-lit night in the Caribbean, where I'd gone to record some new music, I stood under a glittering sky and performed my first active Devotion outside, only inches from the waves surging onto the shore. And something happened that gave me a glimpse of understanding of a spiritual phenomenon at the heart of connection.

AFFIRMATION

It was a warm, Moonless night. Jubilant stars swarmed across the sky. I was standing on a narrow stone promontory, with waves rolling into the shore all around me. The distant horizon was a pale, thin line across the visible world, separating dark sky from darker sea. I was alone, and there was no one nearby.

I said aloud: *When there's a sign of some kind, I'll begin …*

A few seconds later a massive explosion of light flashed on the horizon. It was a violent lightning storm, but it was so far away that I couldn't hear a sound or see anything but the fierce flare of light crashing furiously somewhere in that faraway tempest.

Okay, I said aloud. *Good enough for me …*

I committed my Intention, took a deep breath, raised the conch shell to my lips and blew out a long, strong blast of sound.

I was holding the conch shell in both hands. My index fingers were raised above the shell, providing a little gap of dark space between them.

A meteor suddenly scraped across the sky, moving exactly between my two raised fingers, arcing from my left to my right.

I was stunned and excited, but I kept my focus, and completed that, and the next six conches.

Just before the last conch blow finished, as I was reaching a crescendo with my remaining breath, another shooting star arced between my fingers, moving from right to left this time. The meteor's thin blaze of light was extremely bright and intense, ending just before I ended my conch blow.

I think that was an Affirmation. In fact, after many, many such events, I'm sure that it was.

However, it wasn't the Universe or the Divine Perfection or the Spiritual Reality *sending meteors across the sky as an Affirmation of something to me personally.*

So much of the writing on and from within the spiritual seems, to my critical thinking, to conflate the superstitious with the spiritual.

For the sake of argument, I'm going to say that the superstitious is about perspectives on *belief,* and the spiritual is solely about the *experience of connection* to the Divine Perfection's Spiritual Reality, in whatever formulation that means to you.

Using that distinction, a lot of available literature about the phenomenon known as Affirmation is superstitious, rather than spiritual. In its most simplistic form, this way of looking at the Affirmation phenomenon holds that the natural world *responds to* the seeker on the Path. I don't think that happens. I'm sure that the meteors would've scratched across the sky in the same way, and at the same time, whether I was there or not.

It was an Affirmation because I was in exactly the right place, at exactly the right time, doing exactly what I needed to do be doing, and with exactly the right Intention, *to experience the event as an Affirmation.*

I was in sync with the Spiritual Reality, to the extent that I was in exactly the right place at exactly the right time and with exactly the right Intention for the sync to happen. And when we're in sync, we're primed to experience Affirmations, and they happen all the time.

It's not the Universe consciously telling my Self something specific, so to speak, it's my Self, consciously tuning in to the Universe's constant language of Affirmation.

In that sense, the Affirmation is always about who, when, where and how we are: we're either in the kind of spiritual place or disposition that perceives some of the constant Affirmations, or we're not in that place in our lives; but either way, the Affirmations are always there.

In my few years of experience, Affirmations are not vitally important to evolving progress on the Path. They're not signposts leading the way, so far as I can tell, and in any case, Devotion is its own instruction in refinements of practice, with its own signs. And the Affirmations are not important to anyone but the seeker who perceives them, and almost impossible to articulate to someone else's satisfaction.

But within the long walk on the spiritual Path, and as such Affirmations become ever more frequent and vary from subtle signs to unmistakably vivid and "freakish" events, they seem to me something like Automated Course Corrections in sea and air navigation systems, to stretch a point. Every breakthrough that helps to enhance the Worthiness to perform the practice through sincerity, honesty and authenticity about the Self, and that helps to refine the practice of Giving in Devotion itself, is immediately affirmed, in my experience, by the Affirmation state of the devoted Self.

Some time back, it occurred to me that I should light a candle for the Ancestors during my Devotional practice. Previously, the Ancestors had been represented in my Sacred space through flowers and a photograph of a departed loved one. The candles I'd been lighting were for the ambience, rather than particular people. I suddenly thought: *I'd like to light a candle mindfully for the Ancestors when I'm doing my Devotion ...*

I turned toward the photograph of the departed loved one, and said *I'll buy some more candles, and light one each time now. I'm sorry, that it took me so long to think of it ...*

I picked up the photograph, and my foot trod on a bag of tea-light candles I'd lost behind a curtain, bursting it open on the floor and spilling out candles. The birds in the birdbath outside suddenly went into a furiously happy circus of singing and flapping feathers. And when I sat down with the photograph and a tea-light candle in my hands, and said to myself: *Well, I'll certainly have to light a candle for you now, won't I ...* a box of matches toppled off a shelf and into my lap.

In the Material Reality perspective, it was a simple string of coincidences, fully predictable within the parameters of my home and functional operation.

In the Spiritual Reality perspective, it was an Affirmation that the Intention formed within my Self was providing a connection sufficient to allow *the appreciation of an Affirmation experience.*

To make the point, it's conceivable that had the matchbox fallen onto my lap in a different moment, I might have been annoyed or mildly surprised. But at that precise moment in which it *did* happen, my experience of the event was such that I could smile at the spiritual Affirmation and accept the material coincidence at the same time. Where detectives may begin their investigation with the motive, in the spiritual everything begins with the Intention.

What was my Intention?

My fully formed Giving Intention was to light a candle for the Ancestors, each time I performed my Devotional practice.

That fully formed Intention was already the Outcome, in the Spiritual Reality. The Affirmation didn't *happen to me or for me:* I was simply in a state within which I could *appreciate and experience* the Affirmation.

It seems to me that Affirmations are always a matter of *You Are Here*, rather than *You Are Fantastic.*

I've known people who speak of Affirmations as if they're a kind of spiritual candy. I've known people who assure me that they've received Affirmations that they should do something irrational. I've known people who rely on Affirmations to commit crimes or even just to get out of bed.

It was always a warning for me, and still is, if in any way someone thinks that *the Universe or any spiritual element makes things happen specifically for them.*

In my experience, when people are not grounded in both perceptions, the available spiritual language alone can lead to perceptions that are very misleading.

I've found that humility, even my own small share, is extremely powerful as an intellectual tool, and hasn't steered me in the wrong direction. Humility allows any seeker on the Path to experience the little skip of delight that comes with an Affirmation, and see it from the Material Reality perspective at the same time, without the pride and vanity that makes everything about Me, Me and Me.

Affirmations are not "spiritual breadcrumbs," so to speak, sprinkled by the Universe or the Divine Perfection along the Path to awareness. And they're not pats on the back or signs of reaching some level of attainment: not in my experience.

Affirmations, if they exist at all, must proceed from the language of the Spiritual Reality, which is the language of creative Giving. They can't affirm behavior predicated on selfishness or malice or destructive taking. That would be a logical inconsistency.

It's not about the Universe, coming to you. It's about you, coming to the Universe.

I went out onto a sand-strewn pebble path near the sea to blow the conch. It was a hot afternoon, and it had taken the long walk to that isolated point for my feet to adjust and tolerate the heat on the flagstones.

I was about to brush my feet against the path roughly to remove any sand and grit that had gathered on the walk, when it occurred to me that I'd seen a lot of ants on the pathway, dodging them with my steps, and that perhaps an ant was near my foot and I might unconsciously sweep it to extinction, just by carelessly brushing my feet.

I took a step back, and looked at the space where I had determined to perform my Devotional practice to see if any insects were ambling about. There was an ant there, behaving strangely.

I saw the ant moving around very swiftly in concentric circles. I thought that the hot path might be causing it distress. I said aloud: *Hey, is that path too hot? Would you like some shade?*

I leaned over, casting a cooling shadow on the whirling ant, and hoping that the insect would follow it to a shadier place nearby. It didn't work. The ant scrambled around in circles even more swiftly.

I knelt down and saw that the ant was circling a small piece of jagged glass. It was exactly where I would've scraped my foot harshly to rub off the grit. It was also exactly where I would've pressed down hard with the heel of my foot to keep my Self fully conscious during the blowing of the conch.

I said: *Wow*, in my mind. I wish the thought had been *Thank you*.

The ant immediately widened its perimeter to begin racing to a certain point and then back again, backwards and forwards in a frantic scramble. From my kneeling perspective I looked along the line of sight taken by the ant, and saw dozens of jagged shards of glass.

Someone had dropped a glass, but the shards were almost invisible in the bright sunlight. They were scattered on the path I'd chosen for my return walk, and I would've trodden on them.

This time I did say: *Thank you, Brother Ant*.

The ant scrambled away to the shady patch and disappeared.

I performed my Devotional practice, blowing the conch shell in seven fairly strong, sustained notes.

When I completed the Devotion, I looked around for the ant. I know it sounds weird, but ... I did.

I found the ant, or another ant, whirling in circles again, but this time around a small, glass pyramid I'd brought with me. The first words that sprang from my lips were *So, you like that, do you?*

I reached out to pick up the pyramid and discovered that it was very hot, and at risk of perishing or cracking. The ant trundled off to the shadows. When I left the wild place, I poured a trickle of water near the shady spot for the ant as a small gift of gratitude.

I *know* that it was an Affirmation, *and* a set of coincidences, at the same time

Such interactions happen constantly, but we need to have a special lens through which to experience and perceive them. That special lens is not merely required to apprehend such phenomena; it's required *to even think about them.*

Would the ant have been there, and done that, whether I came along or not?

Yes. Of course. There may have been something about that particular shard of glass refracting and reflecting light on that particularly hot day that compelled the ant to behave that way. Whatever the "explanation," I'm sure that it was a natural phenomenon, and that it would've occurred whether I was there to see it or not.

Was it a coincidence that the very sharp shard of glass was exactly in the place where my foot would've pressed down hard on it, had I not known it was there?

Yes, I think so. My choice of that place to stand, though not arbitrary, could've conceivably been some way to the left or right of that spot.

But I was there, at the right moment, and with the right Intention.

You are the Affirmation, in an Affirmation event.

How many shooting stars does it take to confirm an Affirmation? I've seen more of them since I've been blowing conch under the stars than I have in my entire life, dozens of them, and always at significant Affirmation moments in the performance of my Devotion.

I've seen a golden mongoose, swarms of bats that surrounded me with every blow of the conch but never touched me, a black fox, clouds of butterflies, sudden flocks of birds in an empty sky, a crane dancing at my feet, shoals of fish leaping from the waves between blows of the conch, circling vultures that appear at the start of the set and depart at the end, a hummingbird hovering before my eyes, a firefly that circled my head, crows, hundreds of crows, and many more wonders during Devotion.

In the Material Reality these are all explicable coincidences. In the language of the spiritual they are both coincidences and joyful, significant Affirmations, each Affirmation simply being a perception that can only occur or be experienced in the right place at the right time and with the right Intention.

One warm night in Melbourne I went into my small backyard to perform a ritual of Devotion to the Goddess Tara, one of the many forms of Maa, and among other things, the Goddess of insight and Enlightenment.

My task was to hold a candle up to the new moon and repeat a mantra of Devotion.

As I began to raise the candle, a huge bat flew over the neighboring fence, dipped to touch me on the head softly, and flew off into the night.

An owl hooted nearby as I lifted the candle to the sky. And as I finished the mantra, a possum ran along the fence line, stopped opposite me, bowed or dipped its head at me five times, then scuttled off.

Of course, these are readily explicable events when looked at from the material perspective. My apartment and its little back yard were in the flight path of a colony of bats, and I often watched them streaming overhead. The fact that the migrating season was over and there had been no bats in the sky that night, or any subsequent night, didn't diminish the fact that it was a flight path. Though unusual to hear an owl in the suburbs, it wasn't an exceedingly rare event. And possums do what possums do.

But from the spiritual perspective, the events were astoundingly significant.

In the Hindu tradition, the bat and the owl, among other creatures, are *carriers* of the Goddess, Maa Kali.

Carriers are animals, birds and even insects – the butterfly and the spider are carriers of Maa – that are auspiciously associated with a Deity.

For a very large black bat to swoop and touch my head at the commencement of a ritual for the Goddess, and an owl to hoot at exactly the moment that the candlelight reaches the sky, and a wild creature to acknowledge my Devotion with five bows of the head is both coincidence and beyond coincidence in the language of the spiritual. It is the Affirmation of connection.

Though I had been standing there and thinking for quite a while before commencing, my Intention state allowed me to begin my Devotion at exactly the right time to experience and perceive the events as Affirmations. Bat, owl and possum would have happened, whether I was there or not. I was just in the right state of Intention to perceive and experience them. It's the connection that's affirmed, not me personally. The long process of Acknowledgement

Surrender and Devotion had strengthened my resistance to vanity, and I constantly reminded my Self that no matter how exhilarating or mind-boggling any Affirmation might be, it wasn't about Me, Me & Me as an Ego: it was about being in the appropriate state of Intention.

And the Affirmation of the shooting stars with the first and last conch blows, that night in the Caribbean, was definitely mind-boggling. The timing was too perfect, the placement of the meteors' flashes between my fingers too precise – it was life changing for me. A doorway opened, so to speak, and the Affirmations happened again, and again, and again. And they still do.

That third year of defiance and Affirmation ended in good spirits. Mum was bravely looking forward to a good year to come. Dad's heart seemed to be holding up under the strain. Relations with loved ones were excellent and our projects were advancing, almost without effort, as we found good creative arts partners, and the climactic Affirmation event of the shooting stars reinvigorated my Devotion.

I was in the right state to take my active Devotion into wilder places, and blow the conch beyond idols.

But as that fourth year began so confidently, I was to learn that every good thing and every bad thing that ever happens to us is a test of Faith, and that the quality of our Faith and the Path we manifest can lead us to personal destruction or to the fulfillment of a Sacred duty.

THE FOURTH YEAR

Dad, our beautiful Stepfather of forty-nine years, died in January, following a massive coronary event. In the hour before his cremation, I had the honor of blowing the conch for him, standing at the feet of his open casket.

I did this from instinct or perhaps from some spiritual intuition. I'd had no instruction to blow the conch for him in that way, but I knew within my Self that I simply had to do it.

Only my Mother and my soul mate A. were present. The acoustics of the large, empty viewing room in the funeral parlor bounced the sound of the conch back at us in superb, reverberating effects.

The conch blows were strong and clear. When I finished and we hugged one another, I had the overwhelming sensation that I'd done something right; or better than right, something required.

Mum moved in with us. She wrote in her diary, which she left to us, that she desperately wanted to join her life companion of forty-nine years in death, but that she would wait six months, because she felt that the loss of both Parents in one month would be too great for the family.

Six months later to the day, Mum died, staring straight into my eyes with her last breath. She exhaled once, and then was still. She had just been bathed, and her body was fragrant. Her eyes were radiant jewels, crystal clear and still glittering as I closed them. Her skin was smooth and flawless, like porcelain.

A few minutes after the doctor pronounced death, I blew conch for my Mother there, in the hospital dying room. A nurse, who happened to be from India, stood in the doorway for me, in case anyone was disturbed by the sound. No one was. No one seemed to hear.

And I blew conch for my Mother, and where once there would've been agonies of tears and wretched sobbing, there was instead the long, soft wail of the conch. Where once I would have been consumed with what *I* was feeling, I now had a way to give to her, and in the Giving all my grieving dissolved, and became a gentle, dutiful service of love.

Despite being a Catholic all her life, and having a sincerely devout love for Jesus, my Mother insisted that a large portion of hers and Dad's ashes should be taken to India for immersion in the Sacred river.

If there's any truth in it, that putting our ashes in the holy river means we don't have to come back again, Mum said, I'd like to take that option, if you don't mind, and stay on the other side …

I brought their ashes to Mumbai in my carry-on case, and went directly to the temple. My Parents had met my spiritual teacher several times, and liked him very much. The sincerity of his Devotion in performing rituals had moved Mum to tears every time she'd watched.

As a Brahmin authorized to perform the rituals, he offered to officiate in the extensive rites involved in helping my Parents' souls to achieve *Moksh*, or liberation from the cycle of reincarnation.

The ceremonies took nine long days and nine longer nights. By the final day we were sleepwalking – all except for my teacher, who seemed to gain in vitality with each exhausting ritual he performed.

My last task was to scrape up the spilled funeral ashes that had fallen onto the flagstones beyond the Sacred fire, using only the palms of my hands. It took me seven hours. My knees were blocks of wood at the end of it and I scraped the skin off both palms, but I didn't feel any pain.

My teacher had instructed me: *When you complete the task, wash yourself, return, sit in a chair near the fire, and cry for some time.*

I did.

I washed and sat by the still smoldering fire. I cried it out. When my teacher returned, he gave me the privilege of performing the last blows of the conch to complete the novena of rituals and ceremonies. We were alone. The dogs, cats, parrots, monkeys, snakes and other creatures that live in the temple ashram were all silent and still. The sound of the conch echoed off walls and between the huge granite idols.

I was trancing from the very first blow of the conch. I don't know if I completed a set of seven, or blew nine or more times. I remember finally opening my eyes while blowing the conch and seeing a light shower of rain falling through the open skylights. There was a shuddering crash of thunder, and then my spiritual teacher was hugging me, and I realized that I was crying again.

On the plane home I had a lot of time to think about how different my actions and reactions would've been during that hard and painful year, if I hadn't taken the leap of Faith and walked on the Path.

I'm ashamed to say it, but I know my Self very well, and I think that in my old life, before Devotion, the loss of both Parents in six months would probably have sent me to self-medication in alcohol for a while.

And though I failed in my tasks of caring more than once, I know that I wouldn't have been as strong for my family as I was, and rather than striving for the liberation of my Parents' souls, I would've wallowed in guilt, regret and grief.

The few years that I'd spent on the spiritual Path had prepared me to see the deaths of my Parents not as something that happened to Me, Me & Me, but in terms of being a Self who was worthy of my Sacred duties to them.

Faith is Freedom from fear.

Faith is also Freedom from the most painful emotions arising from attachment.

Faith is about Giving, and in the Faith-filled moments of pure Giving, without asking for anything in return, we are free from the drag of fear or desire.

Faith sustained me through that fourth year in ways that I couldn't have imagined before I took the leap. Mum lived for two and a half years, thankfully, wonderfully, rather than the six months the doctors predicted. I was grateful for every "extra" day that the family had with her, but I never once asked for her recovery in my Devotion.

I wasn't perfect, when Mum was dying. Anyone who has cared for a dying loved one knows how hard it is, how often we stumble in service, and how many little bits of us die with them. But I know in my heart that if I'd lost my Faith, and I'd asked the Divine Perfection for Mum's recovery, I wouldn't have been as strong for the family or my Self. It was the Faith not to ask, and to keep on Giving when every impulse was to fall on my knees and beg, that gave me the strength to perform my duties as a son, brother, father and uncle faithfully, as a Faith-filled Self.

THE FIFTH YEAR

My spiritual teacher assured me that practitioners of the conch frequently lose consciousness during active Devotion, and that he had passed out many times. Still, I was in no way prepared when it happened to me the first time.

The ocean was in front of me, and on both sides. There were trees behind me. Falcons and vultures soared in the baked blue sky above. I completed my set of seven blows of the conch.

I lowered my head in gratitude for completing what I considered to be a more than adequate set of seven in my Devotion. I looked up at the sky one last time, before walking back to my lodgings.

I don't know what happened then.

I woke up some time later, and I couldn't remember who I was, where I was or what I was.

I was in a bizarre space. I wasn't sure if I was on a ceiling looking down, or on the ground looking up. I didn't have any spatial orientation. I could've been floating, or resting on something. I couldn't feel anything.

I was conscious, and conscious of being conscious. Everything was in focus, but I didn't know what anything was.

I was looking at grass, and I knew that I was looking at something, but I didn't know what grass was. I saw rocks, and I knew that I was looking at them, but I didn't know what rocks were. I didn't know anything, and I had no memory of anything at all.

Then I realized that I was thinking, forming questions, and that I was still "me", although I didn't know who "I" was.

It suddenly occurred to me that this was another Reality, which was a strange thought, because I had no memory of any other Reality. My next thought was that I had to learn how to navigate within this new Reality, in order to survive and find a way back to … I didn't know what.

I saw things, entities, shapes moving at the edges of my vision. When I tried to look at them, they vanished, only to appear again at the periphery.

I was scared. Actually, I was terrified for a little while, because I was immobile in a strange world, and I had no memory.

It may sound weird, although perhaps not after reading this far, but in those seconds of terror, I went back to logic, reason and first principles.

Do I exist?

This feeling of fear is so vivid that I must assume there is a Self of some kind feeling it, and a thinking mind asking the question. So, yes, I exist.

What is the extension of my Self?

I literally asked that question, and found my arms and legs through thinking of my potential body's extension, and recognized my body as mine.

What is my relationship to this space?

I sent my thoughts into my body, and felt that my arm, chest, hip, knee and foot were resting on something.

So, this world or dimension, whatever it is, has surfaces.

What is my spatial orientation?

Just asking myself the question allowed me to "see" or *perceive* the grass as *beneath* me, although I still didn't know what grass was.

So, there's an up and there's a down, and I'm on the down, whatever it is.

It helped, but not a lot, because everything else was too strange.

It was as if the "place" I'd found my Self in had a prismatic view of "other places" that I was aware of peripherally, but that I couldn't focus on because I only had spatial references, but none as to meaning, even to the meaning of grass. I couldn't focus thought on "where" I was, because I didn't know what anything was. Or when ...

Where and when did I come from?

Somehow, I knew that I didn't "belong" to that dimension or space, although I couldn't think of anything else, and I had no frame of reference in that strange world. The thought that this had happened to me was unshakeable, and one of my few straws on that uncertain sea.

It was frightening to look into my own mind and see a blank, white slate every time I tried to step outside the logic stairway and actually know something around me, but couldn't remember.

It was also scarily disorienting to see glimpses of a different, fractured reality at the edges of my vision. It was as though I was looking at a slowly turning hologram that showed everything and nothing at the same time.

I felt my heart racing, heightening my sense of fear, or the dread of being stuck in this world forever. I went back to logic again, and surmised that if this relocation to a new dimension happened, and it resulted in this sensory dislocation, maybe I can find a way back.

How did I get here? What was I doing?

With that thought I spoke a single word that broke the spell: *Conch.*

In that second my hand also slid along the grass until I found the conch shell, where it had slipped from my fingers, and as I touched it, I was completely restored. My fingers closed around the conch and I knew where, when and who I was again.

I sprang to my feet fully awake, and walked home feeling refreshed, but my notebook kept me busy for hours that night.

One of the things that helped me to get through that strange experience is that I've had hallucinogenic experiences before, and I didn't lose control during those previous events, no matter how strange the visions. Many years ago, before I consciously walked the Path, a Shaman from Kinshasa introduced me to what he assured me was the mild spiritual experience of his own hallucinogens, and I saw very strange, five-legged things that weren't there for two days, until the effects dissipated.

I'd been through such experiences chemically, and that's unusual, and inadvisable, but nonetheless effective training for the massive disorientation

I experienced in the unconsciousness event that occurred after blowing the conch that day.

A solid thinking system, using logic and scientific principles, is what got me home.

From the beginning I'd tried to fasten my Devotion to the most dispassionate and critical thinking with which I can educate, criticize and constantly question my Self. In moments such as those trance states, it's my rational mind and strengthened Will that provides my anchor.

Did I learn anything significant from the experience? I don't think so. I've gone through it forensically and I asked my spiritual teacher about it, but beyond the feeling of certainty that what I saw is a unique, genuine glimpse of something, rather than one more among many familiar hallucinations, I can't say that anything important emerged that I could communicate.

Nevertheless, the experience was vivid and fearfully disorientating. I've come close to passing out many times since then, but that first shock was so intense that something has always held me back from a second visit to ... the other side of *this* side. I'm curious, of course, but cautious. My teacher once said: *Every step on the Path is accompanied by crocodiles on either side. And rushing into the spiritual leads to a fall into dangerous waters ...*

And from then on, I made sure that I was in a safe place when performing active Devotion outside. The loss of consciousness occurred when I was in a relatively wild place, which I'd sought, and I woke up next to a pile of rocks. If I'd struck my head when I fell, it might've taken my soul mate a long time to find me.

Even after I regained consciousness, I was incapable of crying out for some time. I made a note – one of the few notes I continued to make in that fifth year – to let someone know when I was going to blow the conch in a wild place, and to make sure that the environment is as trance-friendly as possible, with no hard surfaces.

The event also made me realize that while performing my Devotion, I often lost my peripheral awareness, and I became more careful when selecting a wild place to perform.

I wasn't afraid. Faith is freedom from fear. But I took sensible precautions after that slip into another world, and I still do.

In the fifth year I found that every new moon called me to clean the idols and my Sacred space, without once looking at a calendar. Somehow, I always knew instinctively when very auspicious days in the Hindu calendar occurred, and often called my spiritual teacher before he called me. And my devotional practice honed itself, constantly shedding impediments to effective connection.

The Affirmations continued in abundance. I went through a phase of acknowledging each one reverently, and then I began to ignore them and even closed my eyes when blowing the conch under the stars to avoid them altogether. Now I smile at each one, noting them as beautiful streamers or filaments of connection, and then forget them. Until the next one.

The Path manifested the Path. Everything I could need or want to help me in my active Devotion came to me, without asking for it. The family strode on, arm in arm, allowing grief to settle into acceptance and pursuing their many talents.

Our projects came to fruition with ethical partners after years of delays, contracts were signed, I wrote twenty-six songs for a new album, all of them about love and Faith, we recorded music, commissioned videos, started a new company and foundation, found a lovely little home to rent, collaborated with film makers, actors, painters, composers and musicians, and in December, after almost six years in seclusion on the Path, I returned to the grid and public life, carrying a picture of Mum and Dad with me wherever we go, for them to enjoy the ride.

THE VIEW FROM HERE

My spiritual teacher has blown the conch shell for forty years, and his simplest rituals are many times more strenuous than my most arduous effort. He has blown the conch at oxygen-deprived high altitudes in the Himalayas and in deep, secret caves that only a Sacred few may enter. When I completed my first five years, he smiled and said: *It gets hard, from time to time. I remember, year seventeen was a tough one. And year thirty-one – I wouldn't want to do that one again. But it also gets better every time, doesn't it? Wonderfully better. Enjoy it. Be simple, be innocent, and enjoy it …*

It does get better. And it has become so much a part of my conscious and unconscious life that my only desire, should I be awake at my time of death, is that my soul mate's hand should be in my left hand, and the conch shell in my right.

CONNECTION

Connection is the key to everything.

Anything that happens anywhere, from the exchange of a single photon of light to the interactions between galactic clusters, is the result of connection.

When someone is disconnected from their true, inner Self, from loved ones, from positive friends, from the community, from society and from Nature, this can be both cause and effect of its own very deep distress.

Most often, the successful and happy rehabilitation of that person to full independence of thought and action will involve a process of *reconnecting* the person to their true inner Self, to a loved one, then to careful exchanges of trust with positive people, leading to further constructive engagements with the world of others and Nature.

Connection is the key to the spiritual experience as well: connection between the required version of your Self and the subject of your Devotion.

And it seems to me clearly validated that connection, through Devotion, is achieved by Giving to the Divine Perfection, without asking anything in return.

LAST WORDS

What I've learned comes down, or up, to three very important points.

The first is that the Ego is the wall between the Self and connection to the Spiritual Reality. Devotion is a constant struggle to keep elements of the Ego, such as vanity and pride, to the margins of consideration during active practice. Humility is the key.

Humility is the state of Grace inside us, when we do something Selflessly for the pure benefit of someone we love, or anyone at all, or an animal, or an insect, or a plant. Humility is the core of Faith and the filament of spiritual connection.

I realize that although we all know it when we see it, true humility isn't something easy to define. This makes it hard to strive for within our Selves. In my case, I think of my Mother – how hard she worked, how strong she was, how brave and generous she was, how unshakeable was her Faith – and I remember how many and grievous were the times I failed her. I know that my remaining years aren't sufficient to be worthy of her many sacrifices. That helps build the humble muscle.

When I knelt before my Mother for the first time and put my head at her feet, thanking her for my life and all of her love, my active Devotion received a massive charge. Humility is the ultimate strength, I was surprised to discover.

The second insight is that spiritual Devotion is about Giving, not taking or asking.

The third insight is that there are two spiritual questions:

Am I worthy?

How much Giving is in my Intention?

These three – using humility to shed elements from the Ego not required for connection, Giving in Devotion without asking for anything, and constantly asking the two spiritual questions – are the pointer stars from my experiences on the Path that I would pass on to that younger Self, roaming somewhere, everywhere, in search of Truth and connection.

My teacher once said: *I love everyone in the world, but I can only tolerate one percent.*

I've known a lot of very nice people in my wayward life and quite often, sadly, I wasn't one of them: I was just with them, and wishing I were more like them.

If I can say it about my Self, I think I'm a little nicer now, a little more tolerant and patient, more positive and creative, happier, more focused and reliable, and I hope worthy of my loved ones and of friendship. I also know that none of that would have happened, particularly in the face of crisis, without the leap of Faith and the solace of Devotion.

I know, now, what I was searching for, in all those decades of wandering and wondering: I was searching for my devoted Self.

I look to my teacher's example and I know there's a very long way to go on this journey. But the Path … the bliss … the Path is so beautiful, splendored, sublime, adorned and fulfilling.

Please, Maa, just give me the strength to do it again, tomorrow.

Love and Faith

GDR

My Spiritual Teacher

(Photo by GDR)

Guruji Shri Prabir Priyaranjan Bhattacharjee